Jain Story Book

(JAINA Education Series 202 - Level 2)

Compiled by
JAINA Education Committee
Federation of Jain Associations of North America

Jain Story Book - JES 202
(JAINA Education Series 202 - Level 2)
Third Edition (revised): April 2005
ISBN: 1-59406-011-8
Printed in Korea

Please provide us with your comments and suggestions.

Support JAINA Education activities.
Your contribution is tax deductible in USA.

Published and Distributed by:
Federation of Jain Associations in North America

JAINA Education Committee
Pravin K. Shah, Chairperson
509 Carriage Woods Circle
Raleigh, NC 27607-3969 USA
Telephone and Fax - 919-859-4994
Email - education@jaina.org
Websites - www.jaina.org

Use the above address for communication and for availability of the Education books in other countries

Dedicated

to

Young Jains of America (YJA)
(www.yja.org)

Young Jain Professionals (YJP) and
(www.yjponline.org)

Jain Päthashälä Teachers of North America
(www.jaina.org)

for their continued effort and commitment in promoting religious awareness, non-violence, reverence for all life forms, protection of the environment, and a spirit of compassionate interdependence with nature and all living beings. As importantly, for their commitment to the practice of Jainism, consistent with our principles, including vegetarianism and an alcohol/drug free lifestyle.

Our great appreciation to all the Päthashälä Teachers for their effort in instilling the basic values of Jainism, and promoting the principles of non-violence and compassion to all youth and adults.

Special thanks to all Jain Vegan and alcohol/drug-free youth and adults for inspiring us to see the true connection between our beliefs and our choices.

A vegan and alcohol/drug-free lifestyle stems from a desire to minimize harm to all animals as well as to our own bodies, minds, and souls. As a result, one avoids the use of all animal products such as milk, cheese, butter, ghee, ice cream, silk, wool, pearls, leather, meat, fish, chicken, eggs and refrains from all types of addictive substances such as alcohol and drugs.

Acknowledgements

The project of compiling, revising, and editing of the existing JAINA Education series books was accomplished by a dedicated group of Päthashälä teachers, educators, youth, and individuals of North America, India and other parts of the world. The devoted contribution of all these supporters is evident on every page of this series, and is gratefully acknowledged. I would like to extend special thanks to the following people for their notable contribution and support in the publication of the story book.

For Guidance:
Muni Shri Nandighosh-Vijayji M.S.
Muni Shri Ajayasagarji M.S.

For Revising, Compiling, and Editing the Contents:

Pradip & Darshana Shah – Chicago IL
Mukesh Doshi – Chicago IL
Harendra Shah – San Jose CA
Sudhir & Anita Shah – Woodbridge CT
Jadavji Kenia – Dallas TX
Shanti Mohnot – Pittsburgh PA
Alap Shah (Youth Rep.) – Chicago IL
Parul Shah (Youth Rep.) – Raleigh NC
Shweta Shah (Youth Rep.) – Austin TX
Elu Patel (Youth Rep.) – Raleigh NC
Chang Liu (Youth Rep.) – Raleigh NC
Nirav Shah (Youth Rep.) – Woodbridge CT
Rekha Banker – Raleigh NC
Tansukha Salgia – Columbus OH
Neha & Rakesh Jain – Columbus OH
Chandrakant Shah – Chicago IL
Digish and Mamta Doshi – Chicago IL
Indrajit Shah – Chicago IL
Pravin L. Shah – Reading PA
Lata Doshi – Raleigh NC
Vinod Kapashi – UK
Jayasukh Mehta – UK
Arvindbhai Shah – Ahmedabad India

For Cover Design:
Narendra Velani – Chicago IL
Sudhir & Anita Shah – Woodbridge CT

for Layout:
Sudhir & Anita Shah – Woodbridge CT

For Publishing, Printing, Layout, and Distribution Support:
Virendra Shah – Los Angeles CA
Rajendra Mehta – Orlando FL
Lalit Shah – Ahmedabad India
Kusumben Shah – Ahmedabad India

Please pardon me if I have missed any contributors.

Pravin K. Shah, Chairperson
JAINA Education Committee

JAINA Education Series Books
(3RD Edition Revised)

Päthashälä Education Books

Book Number	*Level*	*Age*	*JAINA Education Series Books*	*Status*
JES-101	Level-1	5-9	Jain Activity Book	Printed - Complete
JES-103	Level-1	5-9	Jain Alphabet Book	Printed - Complete
JES-104	Level-1	5-9	Jain Moral Skits	Printed - Complete
JES-201	Level-2	10-12	Jain Sutras and Stavans	Phase 2 review complete
JES-202	Level-2	10-12	Jain Story Book	Printed - Complete
JES-203	Level-2	10-12	First Step to Jainism	Printed - Complete
JES-302	Level-3	13-15	Jain Philosophy and Practice I	Printed - Complete
JES-401	Level-4	16 up	Jain Philosophy and Practice II	Final Review
-----------	Level-1	5-9	Tirthankar Game	Printed - Complete

Reference Books

JES-901	Jainism – Religion of Compassion and Ecology	Printed - Complete
JES-911	Essence of World Religions	Printed - Complete
JES-921	The Book of Compassion (English)	Printed - Complete
JES-922	The Book of Compassion (Gujarati)	Printed - Complete

Preface

Jai Jinendra

Non-violence (Ahimsa) is the backbone and focal point of Jain philosophy. Non-violence, non-absolutistic viewpoint (Anekäntaväda), and non-possessiveness/ non-attachment (Aparigraha) are fundamental principles of Jainism. Non-violence strengthens the proper conduct of every individual, non-absolutistic viewpoints strengthen the right thinking of every individual, and non-possessiveness strengthens the interdependence of all existence and provides harmony in society. If we observe these three principles in their true spirit, peace and harmony can certainly be attained within us as well as in the world.

Although not fully introduced to the western world, Jainism is India's oldest living religion. The basic principles of Jainism are scientific and the 'truths' presented in the Jain scriptures are universal; however, their interpretations and applications have to be done in the context of time and space in which we find ourselves.

In English-speaking countries where many Jains have settled permanently such as USA, Canada, UK, and Africa, children do not have access to Jain educational material. In an attempt to make Jain principles known globally, the educational material must be made widely available in English. It is also necessary to publish Jain literature and educational material in a variety of media (i.e. books, videos, cassettes, CDs, DVDs, and web deployment) for English-speaking people interested in Jain philosophy, religion, and scriptures. JAINA Education committee has taken up this task.

The JAINA Education Committee is pleased to present a set of JAINA Education books (revised 3rd edition) for students of all ages interested in learning Jainism. These books are grouped into four age levels: Level 1 for elementary, Level 2 for middle school, Level 3 for high school, and Level 4 for college students. The entire list of JAINA Education Series Books is listed in this section.

In 1995 and 1997, the first two editions of these books were published by the committee under the leadership of Dr. Premchand Gada of Lubbock, Texas. It took several years of dedicated hard work to compile and publish these series of books. The Jain community of North America has greatly benefited from this effort.

Under a new JAINA Education committee, this 3rd edition series has gone through major revisions incorporating suggestions received from various Päthashälä teachers, educators, and students from different centers. The new committee members are Jain Päthashälä teachers of various centers and they have spent countless hours in the preparation of this

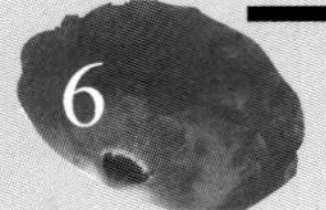

material. Great care has been taken to present the material in a non-sectarian way and incorporate the uniqueness of every Jain sect. Most of the books have been rewritten with the addition of many new topics. Significant effort has been made to maintain consistency in the spellings of Jain words. Many youth have helped us in improving the English grammar in these books.

The Jain Story Book (JES 202 – Level 2) was compiled and coordinated by Pradip and Darshana Shah of Chicago, Illinois. A great deal of effort has been taken by them for the preparation of the material. Significant time was spent in the selection of the stories. The stories were selected from the previous version of JAINA Education story book, the story book by Shri Manubhai Doshi, and few of the stories were gathered from various sources. The education committee members and other supporters have used many sources to compile these stories, and we are grateful to the authors and publishers for being able to use their work liberally. Many adults and youth have helped us to edit these stories such that they meet the objectives of Level 2 students.

Jain scriptures are written using Devanägari characters. To pronounce these characters in English correctly, it is necessary to put various diacritical marks on some English vowels and consonants. However, most internet browsers and word processors do not display and print all these transliterated characters. The main objective of these books is to teach the principles of Jainism to Jain youth and lay people who do not have the knowledge of this transliteration convention. As a result, a simplified diacritical mark scheme has been adopted for this series. The transliteration used here is neither authentic nor totally consistent. While it will serve the purpose of learning Jain principles, this book should not be used for learning correct pronunciations.

The estimated cost of preparation and reprinting this education series will be $75,000. We have received some support in terms of advance payment from various Jain organizations and contributions from various individuals. We need your financial support to complete the project. Please support JAINA education activity generously. We distribute the religious books on a cost basis.

Please note that the JAINA Education committee members are Jain Päthashälä teachers and are not Jain scholars. Hence, you may find some errors in the presentation. Certain items may be applicable to one Jain sect and not applicable to other Jain sects. Please pardon us for any mistakes, oversights, understatements, or overstatements in the material. We request you to use and review the material objectively and provide suggestions to enable us to incorporate them easily in future revisions.

In line with Jain Philosophy, the JAINA education series is not copyrighted. However, if you need to copy and distribute any of the material, please do it respectfully and on a cost basis. Please note that most of these books and other material are available on JAINA Education CD and from the JAINA website - www.jaina.org.

A lot of minds and blessings, both directly and indirectly, have touched this noble project. We sincerely appreciate and thank every person and every organization that made this project successful. As always, if you have any comments and suggestions for improvement, please feel free to contact us.

If we have mentioned anything against the teachings of the Tirthankars, we ask for forgiveness.

Michchhämi Dukkadam.

Pravin K. Shah, Chairperson
JAINA Education Committee
Email - education@jaina.org
Telephone - 919 859 4994
April 28, 2005

Table of Contents

नमस्कारमंत्र	**namaskär mantra**
नमो अरिहंताणं ।	**namo arihantänam |**
नमो सिद्धाणं ।	**namo siddhänam |**
नमो आयरियाणं ।	**namo äyariyänam |**
नमो उवज्झायाणं ।	**namo uvajjhäyänam |**
नमो लोए सव्वसाहूणं ।	**namo loe savvasähünam |**
एसो पंच नमुक्कारो ।	**eso pancha namukkäro |**
सव्वपावप्पणासणो ।	**savvapävappanäsano |**
मंगलाणं च सव्वेसिं	**mangalänam cha savvesim**
पढमं हवइ मंगलं ॥	**padhamam havai mangalam ||**

I bow to Arihantas (Tirthankars), the perfected human souls, who have reached enlightenment by overcoming their inner weaknesses, who have attained infinite knowledge, perception, bliss, and power and have shown the path, which brings an end to the cycle of birth, life, death and suffering.

I bow to Siddhas, the liberated souls, who have attained the state of perfection and immortality by eradicating all karma.

I bow to Ächäryas, who are the head of Jain congregation and preach the principles of religion and show the path of liberation, which is the unity of Right Faith, Right Knowledge, and Right Conduct.

I bow to Upädhyäys who are the ascetic teachers. They explain Jain scriptures and show us the importance of a spiritual life over a material life.

I bow to all Sädhus and Sädhvis who strictly follow the five great vows of conduct and inspire us to live a simple life.

To these five types of great souls, I offer my praise.

Such praise will help diminish my negative vibrations and sins.
Offering this praise is most auspicious of all benedictions.

In short,

I bow and seek inspiration from perfected human souls, liberated souls, enlightened ascetic leaders, ascetic teachers, and all monks and nuns in the world who practice non-violence (Ahimsä), truthfulness, non-stealing, celibacy, and non-possessiveness in their conduct, non-absolutistic viewpoint (Anekäntaväda) in their thinking.

चत्तारि मंगल | chattäri mangalam

चत्तारि मंगलं, अरिहंता मंगलं,	chattäri mangalam, arihantä mangalam,
सिद्धा मंगलं, साहू मंगलं,	siddhä mangalam, sähü mangalam,
केवलिपण्णत्तो धम्मो मंगलं ।	kevalipannatto dhammo mangalam	
चत्तारि लोगुत्तमा, अरिहंता लोगुत्तमा,	chattäri loguttamä, arihantä loguttamä,
सिद्धा लोगुत्तमा, साहू लोगुत्तमा,	siddhä loguttamä, sähü loguttamä,
केवलिपण्णत्तो धम्मो लोगुत्तमो ।	kevalipannatto dhammo loguttamo	
चत्तारि सरणं पवज्जामि,	chattäri saranam pavajjämi,
अरिहंते सरणं पवज्जामि,	arihante saranam pavajjämi,
सिद्धे सरणं पवज्जामि,	siddhe saranam pavajjämi,
साहू सरणं पवज्जामि,	sähü saranam pavajjämi,
केवलि पण्णत्तं धम्मं सरणं पवज्जामि ॥	kevali pannattam dhammam saranam pavajjämi ||

There are four auspicious entities in the universe.
The Arihantas are auspicious.
The Siddhas are auspicious.
The Sädhus are auspicious.
The religion explained by the omniscient is auspicious.

There are four supreme entities in the universe.
The Arihantas are supreme.
The Siddhas are supreme.
The Sädhus are supreme.
The religion explained by the omniscient is supreme.

I take refuge in the four entities of the universe.
I take refuge in the Arihantas.
I take refuge in the Siddhas.
I take refuge in the Sädhus.
I take refuge in the religion explained by the omniscient.

दर्शनं देवदेवस्य, दर्शनं पापनाशनम् ।

दर्शन स्वर्गसोपानं, दर्शनं मोक्षसाधनम् ॥

darshanam devadevasya darshanam päpanäshanam

darshanam svargasopänam darshanam mokshasädhanam ||

The sight of the idol of the Lord, the God of all Gods, is the destroyer of all sins. It is a step toward the heavens, and is a means to the liberation of the soul.

मंगलं भगवान वीरो, मंगलं गौतम प्रभु ।

मंगलं स्थूलिभद्राद्या, जैन धर्मोस्तु मंगलं ॥

mangalam bhagaväna viro, mangalam gautama prabhu |

mangalam sthülibhadrädyä, jaina dharmostu mangalam ||

Bhagawän Mahävir is auspicious, Ganadhar Gautam Swämi is auspicious; Ächärya Sthulibhadra is auspicious; Jain religion is auspicious.

मंगलं भगवान वीरो, मंगलं गौतमो गणि ।

मंगलं कुन्दकुन्दार्यो, जैन धर्मोस्तु मंगलं ॥

mangalam bhagaväna viro, mangalam gautamo gani |

mangalam kundakundäryo, jaina dharmostu mangalam ||

Bhagawän Mahävir is auspicious, Ganadhar Gautam Swämi is auspicious; Ächärya Kunda-kunda is auspicious; Jain religion is auspicious.

अर्हन्तो भगवंत इन्द्रमहिताः, सिद्धाष्च सिद्धिस्थिता ।

आचार्या जिनशासनोन्नतिकराः, पूज्या उपाध्यायकाः ।

श्री सिद्धान्तसुपाठका मुनिवरा, रत्नत्रयाराधकाः ।

पंचै ते परमेष्ठिनः प्रतिदिनम्, कुर्वंतु वो मंगलम् ॥

arhanto bhagavanta indramahitäh, siddhäshcha siddhisthitä |

ächäryä jinashäsanonnatikaräh, püjyä upädhyäyakäh |

shri siddhäntasupäthakä munivarä, ratnatrayäradhakäh |

panchai te paramesthinah pratidinam kurvantu vo mangalam ||

The Omniscients who have been worshipped by heavenly gods; the liberated souls, who are Siddhas; the heads of the religious order who reinforce the four-fold order established by the Jinas; the revered Upädhyäys, well versed in the scriptures; and the Saints, who are also the followers of the true path of liberation (three jewels); may all these five auspicious entities bestow blessings on you everyday.

आदिमं पृथिवीनाथ-मादिमं निष्परिग्रहम् ।

आदिमं तीर्थनाथं च ऋषमस्वामिनं स्तुमः ॥

ädimam prthivinatha-mädimam nisparigraham |

ädimam tirthanätham cha rsabhasväminam stumah ||

We adore Lord Rishabhadev who was the first king, who was the first to renounce all his possessions (everything) and who was the first Tirthankar.

तुभ्यं नमस्त्रिभुवनार्तिहराय नाथ, तुभ्यं नमः क्षीतितलामलभूषणाय ।

तुभ्यं नमस्त्रिजगतः परमेश्वराय, तुभ्यं नमो जिन भवोदधिशोषणाय ॥

tubhyam namastribhuvanärtiharäya nätha |

tubhyam namah ksititalämalabhüsanäya |

tubhyam namastrijagatah parameshvaräya |

tubhyam namo jina bhavodadhishosanäya ||

Lord, bow to you, the eradicator of misery of the three worlds; bow to you the adorable ornament on the face of the earth; bow to you, the Lord of the three worlds; omniscient Lord; bow to you, the destroyer of the sea of the life cycle.

वीरः सर्वसुरासुरेन्द्र-महितो, वीरं बुधाः संश्रिताः

वीरेणाभिहतः स्वकर्म निचयो, वीराय नित्यं नमः ।

वीरात् तीर्थमिदं प्रवृत्तमतुलं, वीरस्य घोरं तपो

वीरे श्री धृति कीर्ति कांति निचयः श्री वीर भद्रं दिश ॥

virah sarvasuräsurendra-mahito, viram budhäh samshritäh

virenäbhihatah svakarma nichayo, viräya nityam namah |

virat tirthamidam pravrttamatulam, virasya ghoram tapo

vire shri dhrti kirti känti nichayah shri vira ! bhadram disha ||

Lord Mahävir is worshipped by all heavenly gods as well as demons; the learned take refuge in Lord Mahävir; the aggregate of his own karmas has been uprooted by Lord Mahävir; I always bow to Lord Mahävir; this unparalleled Tirtha has been set up by Lord Mahävir; Lord Mahävir's austerities were intense; collections of enlightenment (Shri means wealth, here wealth of knowledge), patience, glory, and grace rest in Vir; Oh Lord Mahävir, show me the path to attain bliss.

उपसर्गाः क्षयं यान्ति, छिद्यन्ते विघ्नवल्लयः ।

मनः प्रसन्नतामेति, पूज्यमाने जिनेश्वरे ॥

upasargäh ksayam yänti, chhidyante vighnavallayah |

manah prasannatämeti, püjyamäne jineshvare ||

All the troubles disintegrate, the shackles of obstacles break, the mind achieves a blissful state wherever and whenever the Lord Jineshvars are worshipped.

शिवमस्तु सर्वजगतः, परहितनिरता भवन्तु भूतगणाः ।

दोषाः प्रयांतु नाशं, सर्वत्र सुखीभवतु लोकः ॥

shivamastu sarvajagatah, parahitaniratä bhavantu bhütaganäh |

dosäh prayäntu näsham, sarvatra sukhibhavatu lokah ||

May the entire universe attain bliss; may all beings be oriented to the interest of others; let all faults be eliminated; and may people be happy everywhere.

खामेमि सव्वजीवे, सव्वे जीवा खमंतु मे ।

मित्ती मे सव्व भुएसु, वेरम् मज्झं न केणइ ॥

khämemi savvajive, savve jivä khamantu me |

mitti me savva bhuesu, veram majjham na kenai ||

I forgive all souls; let all souls forgive me. I am on friendly terms with all. I have no animosity towards anybody.

Part I
Tirthankars

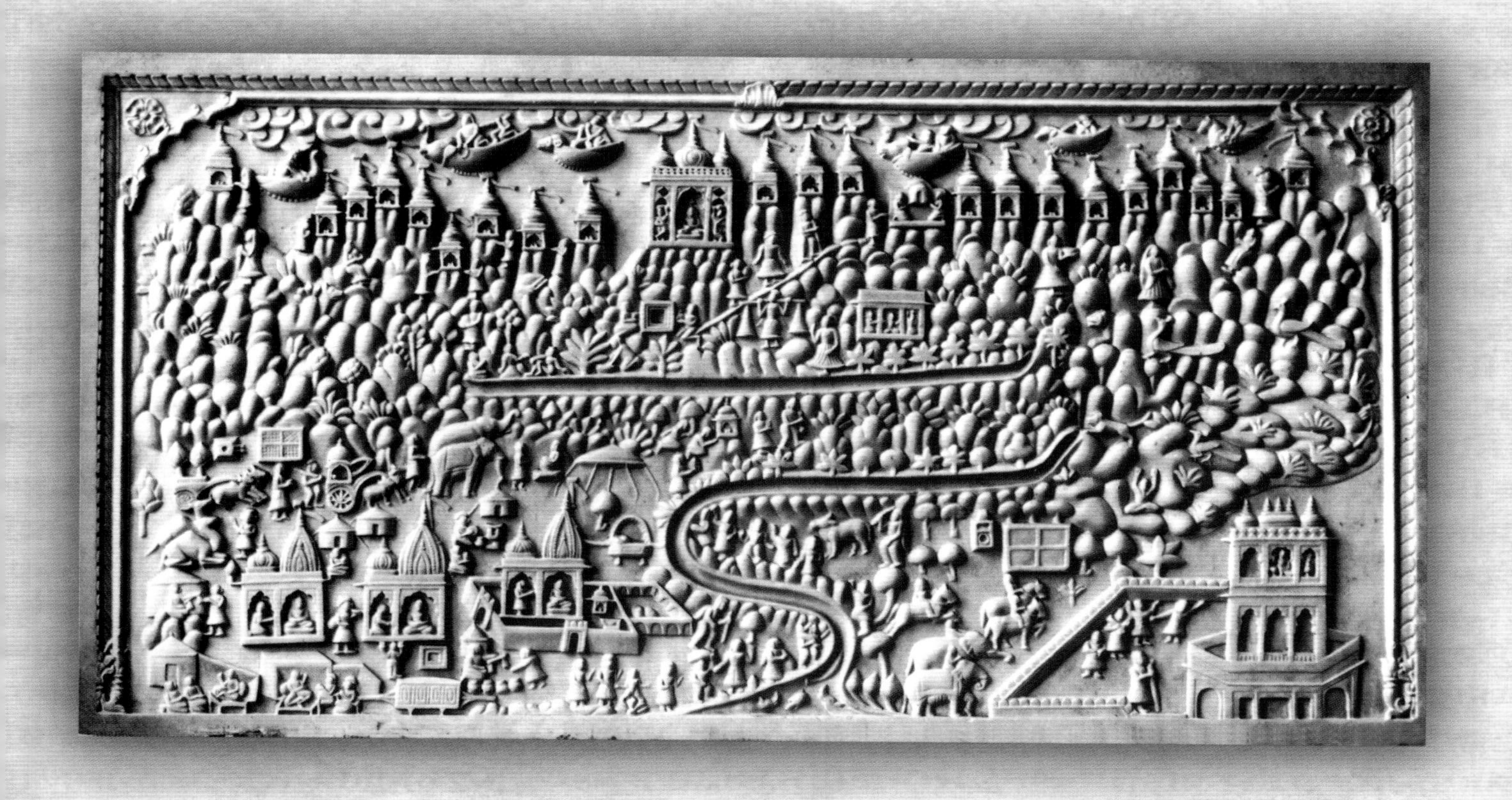

In Jain religion, there are twenty-four Tirthankars. According to Jain philosophy, all Tirthankars were human beings once, but they have now attained a state of perfect enlightenment through meditation and self-realization. They are faultless human models. They are known as the "Gods" of Jains. The concept of a supernatural God as creator, protector, and destroyer of the universe does not exist in Jainism. But Jains pray to these Tirthankars because they show the path to Enlightenment and Liberation.

Only the one who has
transcended fear
can experience equanimity
- Sutrakritäng

01 Bhagawän Mahävir

Bhagawän Mahävir delivering sermon from Samavasaran

About 2600 years ago, religion in India took on a very ugly turn. The management of the original four classes of society - Brahmins, Kshatriyas, Vaishyas, and Shudras had deteriorated. Brahmins were learned people and considered themselves to be very superior. The fate of Shudras or untouchables was terrible and they were required to serve the other castes forever performing the most degrading tasks. They were not allowed to engage in other professions. The importance of sacrifices as a symbol of giving up and renouncing had been misconstrued and it had taken on a very violent form. Animal sacrifices were performed regularly and people believed that these sacrifices would please the Gods and in return their wishes would be fulfilled.

Under such social and religious conditions, Mahävir was born in the month of Chaitra on the 13th day of the waxing (increasing in size) cycle of the moon in 599 BC as per the Indian calendar. This day falls in the month of April and is celebrated as Mahävir Janma Kalyänak day. He was born in the region known as Kshatriya-kund or Kundalpur in the present-day state of Bihar, India. His parents were King

Siddhärtha and Queen Trishalä. Queen Trishalä was the sister of King Chetak, the King of Vaishäli. Bhagawän Mahävir had an older brother named Nandivardhan and a sister named Sudarshanä. The family's prosperity started increasing ever since Queen Trishalä conceived Bhagawän Mahävir, so they named him Vardhamän, which means to "increase".

Birth celebration of Bhagawän Mahävir by 56 female celestial beings

From his early childhood he was intelligent, affectionate, and compassionate. At school he hardly needed any instruction. He excelled in all his subjects. He also proved to be quite fearless. Once when he was playing with his friends, a big snake appeared in the field. His friends were scared and ran away when they saw the snake but Vardhamän was unafraid. He caught the snake and put it in the nearby trees. On another occasion a giant monster came to frighten him but Vardhamän was unmoved. He was popularly known as Mahävir (very brave) since he showed a high level of courage and fearlessness.

At an early age, he realized that worldly happiness and pleasures do not last forever and are based mostly on the inconvenience, miseries, and unhappiness of others. He therefore planned to renounce his worldly life, his possessions, and worldly pleasures in search of true spiritual happiness. However, he knew that his parents would be very sad and hurt if he did this so he decided not to renounce his current life while they were still alive. His parents passed away when he was 28 years old. He was now ready to renounce his worldly life by giving up his family, friends, and possessions; but again postponed it for two more years at the request of his older brother, Nandivardhan. During this period he donated all his wealth to the poor and the needy.

Finally, at the age of 30, he renounced his worldly life and became a monk. Mahävir spent the next twelve and a half years in deep silence and meditation to conquer his desires, feelings, and attachments. He carefully avoided harming or annoying other living beings including animals, birds, and plants. During this time he also observed severe austerities, fasting most of the time, moving bare feet from place to place, and facing all types of hardships peacefully.

During this meditation period of twelve and a half years:

- He faced a fierce and poisonous snake, Chandkaushik, and calmed him down with his compassionate approach
- He suffered peacefully when a farmer put nails in his ears
- He accepted food from a house-maid, named Chandanbälä, to break his approximately 6 month long fast
- He endured all adverse conditions and hardships caused by uncivilized people with patience and forgiveness

During this period, he progressed spiritually and ultimately destroyed all four destructive (Ghäti) Karmas. In doing so, he realized perfect perception, perfect knowledge, perfect power, and perfect bliss. This realization known as Keval-jnän (omniscience or perfect enlightenment). Now, Mahävir became Bhagawän Mahävir or Mahävir-swämi. Bhagawän Mahävir spent the next thirty years traveling bare feet throughout India preaching the eternal truth that he had realized.

He attracted people from all walks of life, rich and poor, kings and commoners, men and women, princes and priests, touchables and untouchables. In matters of spiritual advancement, Bhagawän Mahävir envisioned that men and women were equal. The lure of renunciation and liberation attracted women as well. Many women followed Mahävir's path and renounced the world in search of the ultimate truth and happiness. He categorized his followers into a fourfold order: monks (Sädhus), nuns (Sädhvis), laymen (Shrävaks), and laywomen (Shrävikäs). This order is known as the Jain Sangha.

Bhagawän Mahävir's sermons were compiled orally in 12 books in the form of Sutras by his immediate disciples. These books are called Anga Ägam Sutras. Later, several learned Ächäryas (Shruta Kevali Monks) compiled many more books to further explain the Anga Ägam Sutras. All these books are called Ägams or Ägam Sutras and are considered as the scriptures of Jain religion. These Ägam Sutras were passed on orally to future generations of ascetics. Over the course of time some of the Ägam Sutras were lost. Approximately one thousand years later the memorized Ägam Sutras were organized and recorded on Tädpatris (palm leaves used as paper to preserve records for future references).

The ultimate objective of His teaching was how to attain total freedom from the cycle of birth and death and achieve a permanent blissful state. This blissful state is also known as liberation, nirvana, absolute freedom or Moksha.

This state is achieved when we get rid of our Karmas. We accumulate Karma through our vices such as anger, ego, deceit, and greed. Under the influence of Karma, the soul seeks pleasure in materialistic belongings and possessions. This is the deep-rooted cause of selfishness, anger, hatred, greed, violent thoughts & deeds, and other such vices. These result in further accumulation of Karmas. Bhagawän Mahävir preached that Right Faith (Samyag-Darshan), Right Knowledge (Samyag-Jnän), and Right

Conduct (Samyag-Chäritra) together form the real path to get rid of Karmas which are attached to the soul.

At the heart of right conduct, lie the five great vows:

Non-violence (Ahimsa)	Not to cause harm to any living beings
Truthfulness (Satya)	To speak only the harmless truth
Non-stealing (Achaurya)	Not to take anything that is not properly given
Celibacy (Brahmacharya)	Not to indulge in sensual pleasures
Non-possession/Non-attachment (Aparigraha)	Complete detachment from people, places, and material things

Jains hold these vows as the guiding principles of their lives. These vows can be fully implemented only with the acceptance of the philosophy of non-absolutism (Anekäntaväda). Monks and nuns follow these vows strictly and totally, while Shrävaks and Shrävikäs (lay followers) follow the vows as far as their ability and desire permits.

If the principles of Jainism are properly understood and faithfully adhered to they will bring contentment, inner happiness, and joy in the present life. This will elevate the soul in future reincarnations to a higher spiritual level, ultimately achieving perfect enlightenment.

At the age of seventy-two (527 B.C.), Bhagawän Mahävir attained Nirvana and his purified soul left his mortal body and achieved complete liberation. He became a Siddha, a pure consciousness, a liberated soul, living in a state of complete bliss forever. This event, known as Nirvana, occurred on the last day of the Hindu and Jain calendar. We celebrate it as Diwäli or Deepävali (festival of lights).

Significant points of the Teachings of Bhagawän Mahävir:

Mahävir-swämi made religion simple and natural, and free from elaborate ritual complexities. His teachings reflected the internal beauty and harmony of the soul.

Mahävir-swämi taught the significance of human life and stressed the importance of a positive attitude in life.

Bhagawän Mahävir's message of non-violence (Ahimsa), truth (Satya), non-stealing (Achaurya), celibacy (Brahmacharya), and non-possession/non-attachment (Aparigraha) is full of universal compassion.

Bhagawän Mahävir said, "A living body is not merely an integration of limbs and flesh, but it is the abode of the soul which has the potential for infinite knowledge (Anant-Jnän), infinite perception (Anant-Darshan), infinite happiness (Anant-Sukha), and infinite power and energy (Anant-Virya)." Mahävir's message reflects the freedom and spiritual joy of living beings.

Mahävir-swämi emphasized that all living beings, irrespective of their size, shape, form, and level of spiritual development are equal, and that we should love and respect them all. In this way, he preached the gospel of universal love.

Mahävir rejected the concept of God as a creator, protector, and destroyer of the universe. He also denounced the worshiping of gods and goddesses as a means of material gain and personal benefits.

Bhagawän Mahävir's last sermon at Päväpuri

Jainism believes that any human being is capable of attaining Liberation. A Liberated soul is called Siddha or God. Bhagawän Mahävir is the 24th and last Tirthankar of this era. Bhagawän Mahävir's message of non-violence (Ahimsa), truth (Satya), non-stealing (Achaurya), celibacy (Brahmacharya), and non-possession/non-attachment (Aparigraha) is full of universal compassion. Bhagawän Mahävir propagated the concept of multiplicity of viewpoints known as Anekäntaväda. As all Tirthankars do, Bhagawän Mahävir revived and reestablished the Jain religious order (Jain Sangha) which flourishes to this day. Bhagawän Mahävir's preachings are compiled in several scriptures, collectively known as the Ägam-sutras or Ägams.

02 Bhagawän Ädināth

Time is infinite where there is no beginning or end. It continuously migrates from periods of progress to periods of decline, and one period follows another. According to Jain tradition, a period of progress, known as Utsarpini or the ascending order, is marked with all around improvements such as longer life span, prosperity, and overall happiness. On the other hand, a period of decline, known as Avasarpini or the descending order, is marked with all around deterioration and decline such as a shorter life span, and general gloom. These two periods together make one time cycle.

Each Utsarpini and Avasarpini is divided into six eras called Äräs, meaning the spokes of a wheel. The present time is the fifth Ärä of the Avasarpini period. It is also known as Dusham (Unhappy) Ärä. Hindu tradition calls it Kaliyuga.

Until the end of the third Ärä of the current Avasarpini, people were leading a more natural and simple life. The population was small and nature was bountiful. Nature provided all the necessities for human beings so they did not have to exert much effort for obtaining the necessities of life. Trees provided shelter and enough leaves and bark for covering their bodies. With the help of the branches, they could erect huts for protection from rain and extreme weather. When they felt hungry, they could pick their food from the trees and bushes. There was enough flowing water for cleaning their bodies and quenching their thirst. As such, there was no struggle for existence or rivalry for survival, and people spent their lives in peace.

The people lived in tribes and had a leader known as a Kulkar or king. Towards the end of the third Ärä, there lived a Kulkar named Näbhiräyä. He could peacefully manage the community of that time. In due course, his beautiful wife, Queen Marudevi, gave birth to Rishabha.

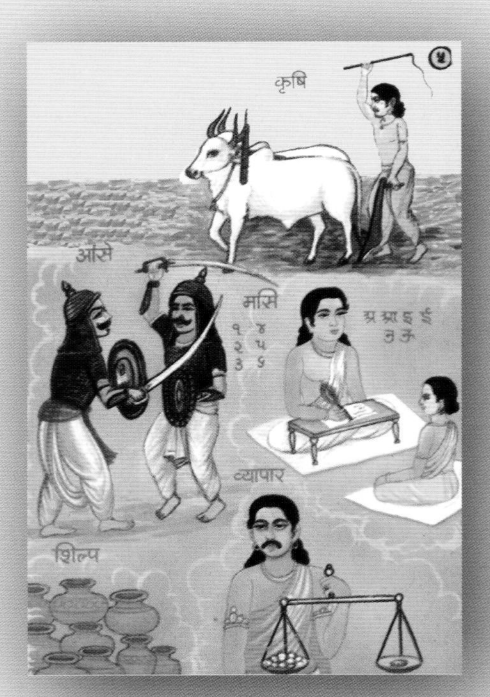

Rishabhadev teaching life skills and trades

The world's conditions started changing after Rishabha was born. There was an increase in population and nature no longer remained as bountiful as it used to be. This gave rise to a struggle for the acquisition and accumulation of the necessities of life. A sense of jealously and envy also arose in its wake. Näbhiräyä, as the leader of the community, tried to restrain the struggle to the utmost possible extent. In due course, as Rishabha grew to be a bold, intelligent, and enthusiastic young man, Näbhiräyä entrusted the management of the kingdom to him.

Rishabha was a visionary, a thinker, and an inventor. He foresaw that the struggle for survival would become worse unless some system of producing the necessities of life was created. He realized that people could make an effort for obtaining what they need from nature instead of relying exclusively on natural bounties. Being the genius that he was, he evolved the art of crop cultivation and taught people how to grow food and fiber. Thus, he ushered in what we call the age of material civilization.

To make the lives of people more comfortable, he taught them how to make utensils, cook food, build houses, make clothes, cultivate land, and to raise animals like cows and horses. He also developed different arts and crafts whereby a variety of articles could be made from wood, metal, and stone. Thus the first city named Vinita came into existence. This city was later known as Ayodhyä.

Rishabha was married to Sumangalä and he was also married to another woman named Sunandä who had lost her husband. Rishabha sanctified the system of marriage and institutionalized family life. Thus, a social order was evolved and Rishabha, as the first acknowledged ruler of human society, came to be known as King Rishabhadev. He ruled for a very long time and laid down equitable rules and regulations for ensuring peace and safety within his realm. People of the kingdom loved Rishabhadev for providing peace and happiness.

Rishabhadev marrying Sunandä and Sumangalä

Rishabhadev had 100 sons. The eldest two, Bharat and Bähubali, were well known. He also had two daughters, Brähmi and Sundari. These four children were experts in different arts and crafts. Bharat became a brave warrior and a capable ruler. Jain literature indicates that India was named 'Bhärat' after him. Bähubali, true to his name (Bähu means arm and Bali means mighty), was known for his exceptional arm strength. Brähmi was a very educated girl. She evolved the art of writing and developed the Brähmi script in which most of the scriptures were written. Her sister, Sundari, cultivated an exceptional talent in mathematics.

Rishabhadev had every reason to be proud and happy with his achievements. However, one incident occurred to make him change his way of thinking. Once while he was watching a dance, the dancer suddenly collapsed and died. Rishabhadev became very disturbed by this incident. He started pondering over the death of the dancer and realized that every phenomenon and every situation in the universe undergoes changes and that no situation remains permanent. He decided to renounce worldly life in search of lasting happiness and distributed his kingdom among his children. He gave Bharat the city of Vinita and entrusted the city of Taxshilä to Bähubali. To the remaining 98 sons, he distributed other parts of his vast kingdom. Then, he renounced all his possessions and became a monk in search of the ultimate truth. Four thousand of his associates and followers also joined him in renunciation.

As a monk, Rishabhadev traveled from place to place. He remained in a state of continuous meditation and did not think of food or water. Since Rishabhadev remained deeply immersed in meditation he could not guide his followers on how they should live their life as monks. His followers could not fast like him and they did not want to go back. They were confused and started behaving on their own accord. . They decided to live on fruits and vegetables obtained from the nearby jungles.

After sometime, Rishabhadev could see their miserable condition. Jain monks are not supposed to pick any fruits and vegetables from trees by themselves but go to laypeople's house for alms (for food). He therefore decided to demonstrate the way a monk is supposed to live. Rishabhadev started going from house to house for alms in silence. However, people did not know what to offer Rishabhadev who was

Shreyäns offering sugarcane juice to Rishabhadev

once their beloved king. They offered him ornaments, their homes, and other valuable items but no one thought of offering food. As a result, Rishabhadev had to continue fasting day after day.

After undergoing fasts for 400 days (thirteen months and nine days), Rishabhadev passed by a sugarcane farm located near the town of Hastinäpur. The farm belonged to his great grandson, Shreyäns. He offered sugarcane juice to his Great Grandfather. Thus, Rishabhadev ended his long fast with sugarcane juice. It was the third day of the bright half of the month of Vaisakha known as Akshaya Tritiya day. This day usually falls in the month of May. In commemoration of this event, people observe a similar austerity known as Varsitapa for 400 days. As it is not possible for people to fast that long, they fast on alternate days; and at the end of 400 days, they break their fast with sugarcane juice on Akshaya Tritiya (Akhätrij) day.

After years of rigorous austerities and the search for truth, Rishabhadev attained Keval-jnän while meditating under a banyan tree on the 11th day of the dark half of Falgun (which usually falls in March). This is known as the ultimate enlightenment and the attainment of Omniscience. In order to guide people towards the right path, he established the fourfold religious order comprising of monks (Sädhus), nuns (Sädhvis), laymen (Shrävaks), and laywomen (Shrävikäs). This order is known as the Jain Sangha.

Rushabhsen, the son of King Bharat became the head of the monks and Brähmi and Sundari headed the order of nuns. As a founder of the religious order known as Tirtha, Rishabhadev is the first Tirthankar of the current Avasarpini part of the time cycle. Thus being the first Tirthankar or Lord, he is also known as Ädinäth (Ädi means the first or the beginning and Näth means the Lord). Thereafter he lived long and taught the truth about everlasting happiness.

Along with the rules of ascetic life, Bhagawän Rishabhadev taught the noble and moral ways of a householder's life. The popular Jain period of austerity, known as Varsitapa, is observed in commemoration of the 400 days of fasting that Rishabhadev did before receiving food from a layperson. Offering pure food to a Sädhu is one of the noblest acts for a layperson. In this manner, even if we cannot follow the ascetic life, we can show our reverence by offering food to a Sädhu. Our scriptures have praised Däna Dharma (donation) of Shreyäns generously.

03 Bhagawän Mallinäth

A long time ago King Mahäbal ruled over the city of Veetshoka in Mahä-videha region of Jambudvipa. King Mahäbal had six very close childhood friends. All seven of them were so close that they did everything together. None of them did anything without seeking the advice of the others.

Prince Mahäbal and six friends

Once a well-known Ächärya named Dharmaghosh-suri came to Veetshoka city. King Mahäbal and his friends went to listen to his sermon and were very impressed. Mahäbal realized that extreme misery and pain exists in living a worldly life. He decided to renounce worldly life and shared his desire with his friends. His friends also agreed to renounce their worldly life along with him. King Mahäbal and his six friends became monks and disciples of Dharmaghosh-suri.

As monks, these seven friends observed austerities and restraints together. Unknown to his friends however, Mahäbal sought more than just freedom from the pains of worldly life. He had an intense desire to make every living being free from suffering and to guide them towards liberation. This desire leads to the acquisition of the Tirthankar-Näm-Karma. To achieve his objective, Mahäbal secretly observed longer austerities. Because of this intense penance, Mahäbal acquired Tirthankar-Näm-Karma. At the same time, because of this secrecy he acquired the karma that he would be born as a female in the future.

All of them continued to observe ever-increasing austerities throughout their lives. At the end of their lives, all of them attained a heavenly abode. After completing the heavenly life span, Mahäbal and his six friends were born as human beings in different places.

During this time King Kumbha was ruling over the city of Mithilä, India. He had a Queen named Prabhävati. She was pregnant and saw 14 (16 by the Digambar tradition) pious dreams indicating the arrival of a Tirthankar soul. Since Mahäbal had earned the Tirthankar-Näm-Karma and a female gender his soul descended into the womb of Prabhävati and was born as Princess Malli. (The Digambar tradition believes that Tirthankar Mallinäth was male and rejects the acquisition of female gender Karma). A few years later, Queen Prabhävati had a son named Malladin.

The six friends of Mahäbal were reborn as princes in different kingdoms and in due course became powerful kings of the cities of Hastinäpur, Ayodhyä, Champä, Käshi, Kämpilypur, and Shrävasti. All these cities were located in the present states of Uttar Pradesh and Bihar.

King Kumbha and Queen Prabhävati lovingly raised their children Malli and Malladin. Princess Malli was exceedingly charming and beautiful and grew up to be a very attractive girl. Malladin respected his elder sister. King Kumbha wanted to give them the best education and therefore entrusted their training to highly respected teachers who taught them all the required arts and crafts. Princess Malli mastered all the fine arts and became a very talented and accomplished princess. Malladin learned all the martial arts and became a bold and brave youth.

King Kumbha decided to establish an art gallery in Mithilä. A marvelous building was constructed for this purpose and all the well-known artists were invited to make their artistic contribution to the gallery. An artist from Hastinäpur had an exceptional ability and possessed a special power to prepare an accurate portrait of anyone by merely seeing one part of his or her body. He once happened to see the toe of princess Malli and from that, he drew an accurate portrait of princess Malli on the wall. The portrait was excellent and displayed every minute detail of the princess. It was so lifelike that when prince Malladin came to see the gallery and looked at the portrait he felt as if his sister was standing there and actually folded his hands as a token of respect.

When he realized that it was merely a portrait, he was puzzled as to how the artist had obtained such minute details of his sister's body. He was told of the special power and the talent that the artist possessed. It was no doubt a very rare accomplishment. However, the prince foresaw the dangers of such talent. He therefore wanted to prevent the use of that special power. The artist was asked to abandon his art in return for a suitable reward. The artist refused and insisted upon his freedom of artistic expression. In order to prevent the misuse of the artist's talents the prince ordered that the thumb of the artist be cut off. The artist was very angry and displeased and decided to take revenge.

The angry artist returned to Hastinäpur without one thumb. He found another artist who could draw a portrait of princess Malli according to his instructions. In time he prepared a yet more attractive portrait of Malli and presented the portrait to the king of Hastinäpur (who was once Malli's close friend in their previous life). The king was very impressed by the portrait. He fell in love with Malli and decided to make princess Malli his wife. He sent a marriage proposal to King Kumbha of Mithilä.

In the same manner the kings of Ayodhyä, Champä, Käshi, Kämpilypur and Shrävasti also learnt of the exceptional beauty of princess Malli and all of them sent their proposals to marry her. After considering these proposals, King Kumbha did not find any of the proposals suitable for Malli and rejected them all. This angered the six kings and they decided to conquer the city of Mithilä in order to get princess Malli. King Kumbha boldly faced them with all his might but he could not withstand the combined strength of the invading forces. He retreated back to his kingdom and closed the gates of the city. The invading forces then laid siege on Mithilä. The city could not withstand the siege from the six kingdoms. This was indeed a big problem.

When princess Malli came to know of the situation and the problem she contemplated on the issue. Gifted with an enlightened mind, she realized that the root cause of the problem lay in her earlier life. She recalled her life as King Mahäbal and all the events of that life. She realized that due to their deep affection for her in their previous life all the six kings coveted to be near her.

Malli decided that since she was the cause of the problem she should find a solution. She requested her father not to worry and leave everything to her. She remembered that the palace had a hall with six doors. Behind each door she arranged beautifully furnished rooms. The doors of the hall were fitted with a fine screen through which people sitting in the rooms could look into the hall but they could not see what was happening in the other five rooms.

Six kings looking at the statue of Malli

Princess Malli commissioned a lifelike statue of herself so that anyone looking at the statue would believe that it was the princess herself. The inside of the statue was hollow with a hole at the top, which could be covered tightly. The statue was placed in the middle of the hall and a maidservant was asked to put a morsel of food twice a day within its cavity and to close its top immediately.

Then she requested her father to send invitations to all six kings to come to the hall to meet her. The plan was to invite them to the hall in the evening and have them wait in the room assigned to them. At the appropriate time all the kings came and occupied their respective rooms. As they glanced through the screen they immediately noticed the beautiful statue of Malli. Each of them thought it was Princess Malli herself and anxiously waited to go inside. They also noticed that Malli was far more beautiful than they had expected and fell more deeply in love with her.

As they were waiting, princess Malli entered the hall through a secret tunnel and standing behind the statue opened the top. The food that was put in the statue had rotted and emitted a foul odor. The smell was so obnoxious that the kings had to cover their nose. Thereupon Malli presented herself and asked why they could not stand the smell of the person whom they loved so much. They admitted that they could not bear the foul odor.

Malli then explained that the food she ate was the same food in the statue. The food in her body did not stink because her soul prevented the rotting. However, when her soul would leave the body, her body too would start to decay. It is the nature of the body to degenerate, decay, and disintegrate. Malli asked the kings, "What is the purpose of being attached to a body when it is destined to rot eventually? Is it not worthwhile to pursue something that will last forever?"

As the kings stood there in amazement, she explained that they were seven very close friends and had done everything together. Upon hearing this they recalled their past lives and what they had renounced. This raised an acute sense of detachment for the short-lived worldly life. All of them decided to renounce the world in order to enhance their spiritual pursuit that they had left undone in the earlier life.

Very elaborate arrangements were made for the renunciation ceremony of Princess Malli. She gave up everything and adopted self-initiation at a place known as Sahasrämravan. She destroyed all of her destructive Karma (Ghäti Karmas that affect the nature and quality of the soul) in a very short time and attained Keval-jnän (omniscience) on the very same day. She became the 19th Tirthankar of the Jain religion. Thereafter she traveled throughout the country for a long time to show the path of liberation to others. Ultimately, she attained liberation on Mount Sametshikhar.

The Shvetämbar tradition believes that Tirthankar Mallinäth was a female and the other 23 Tirthankars were male. Idols of Tirthankars represent the qualities of the Arihantas and not their physical body. Hence, the physical appearance of the idols of all the Tirthankars is the same without any indication of male or female gender.

This body is a mere vessel that holds the soul. Upon death, the soul simply moves to another body unless one attains liberation from the cycle of birth and death. One needs to realize that this veil of skin and flesh is mortal. Physical beauty is deceptive and temporary. Princess Malli made this point through the statue and the rotten food. The importance of our human life is that it is a means of attaining liberation from the cycle of birth and death. One needs to rise above the physical aspects of life and use this life to progress spiritually so that the soul can attain liberation.

04 Bhagawän Neminäth

Long time ago the Yädava clan had settled on the banks of the River Yamunä in India. Mathurä and Sauripura were the major centers of the Yädava community. They are located in the present-day state of Uttar Pradesh. The Yädava king, Samudravijay, was ruling over Sauripura with his wife, Shivädevi. Lord Neminäth was born to them and was named Nemkumär. When he was in his mother's womb, she dreamt of a series of black jewels, called Arista. He is therefore also known as Aristanemi.

King Väsudev, the younger brother of king Samudravijay was the king of Mathurä. He had two queens. Queen Rohini had a son named Balräm (Padma) and Queen Devaki had a son named Shri Krishna. Both Balräm and Shri Krishna were the ninth Baldev and Väsudev as per Jain tradition. Shri Krishna is the incarnation of Lord Vishnu (God) in Hindu religion.

During this time hunting was a favorite sport and gambling was considered a respectable activity. Animals were sacrificed on the altar in religious ceremonies, and non-vegetarian diet was very popular.

Also at this time, the whole area of central India had been disturbed due to the prevailing conspiracies among various kingdoms. King Kamsa and the oppressive king Jaräsangha of Magadha were the worst. King Jaräsangha was Prativäsudev as per Jain tradition.

In order to protect the people and get away from these everyday problems, various kings of the Yädava clan, including Samudravijay, Väsudev, Ugrasen, and Shri Krishna migrated from Mathurä and Sauripura to the West Coast of Gujarat, India. Shri Krishna constructed the large and beautiful town of Dvärkä on the seacoast near the Raivatak (Girnar) Mountain. Its grand architecture and strong fortification made it heavenly, beautiful and unconquerable.

Ugrasen became the king of Junagadh, situated on the other side of the foothills of Mount Girnar. By his wife Dhärini, he had a daughter named Räjimati or Räjul. She was a very beautiful and graceful young girl. Many princes were eager to marry her. However, when she came to know of Nemkumär she became captivated by him and desired to marry him. King Ugrasen sent a request of Räjul's engagement to Nemkumär. After considerable effort, friends and family persuaded Nemkumär to become engaged to Räjul. With much hesitation, he agreed. Everyone was happy as Nem and Räjul would make an ideal couple. The two were engaged and an auspicious day was fixed for their wedding ceremony.

Nemkumär's wedding procession

For King Ugrasen, the wedding of his beloved daughter was a once in a life time occasion. He made elaborate wedding arrangements. On the wedding day, a large number of people joined the gorgeous wedding ceremony. Nemkumär mounted his chariot, specially decorated for the wedding. When the procession was approaching their destination, he heard the sobbing sounds of animals. Moreover, on the side of the road, he saw large fenced areas and cages full of wailing animals and birds. Filled with sympathy and compassion, he asked the charioteer why those animals and birds were kept in bondage.

The charioteer informed him that the wailing sound was coming from the birds and animals that were to be slaughtered for the wedding dinner. Nemkumär could not bear the idea of violence being caused on the account of his wedding. He asked the charioteer to free all the animals and birds. He started thinking about how to prevent such violence. 'Can there be a way of life that would extend peace and security to every living being?' he asked himself. As he thought deep into the matter, it was clear to him that he should explore a way for the well-being of all. He visualized that after marriage he might get too involved in worldly life. Then it would be hard for him to embark upon such an exploration. He realized that the present was the right time for him to explore the truth that would lead to the happiness of every living being. Therefore, he decided not to get married.

All the animals and birds are released at Nemkumär's request

Everyone on the bridegroom's side was taken aback by his decision. His friends and close relatives tried to dissuade him from his decision. He calmly explained that his mission was to explore freedom from misery for all living beings. He further explained that, "As these animals were prisoners in their cages, we all are prisoners in the cages of Karma which are much stronger than these fences. The feeling of joy is evident in the animals released from the cages. Happiness is in freedom, not in bondage. I want to find the path of breaking this bondage of Karma and embrace eternal bliss. Please do not stop me." Then he asked the charioteer to turn back.

After returning to his kingdom, Nemkumär spent one year donating all his belongings to the poor and the needy and then left his royal palace and went to the nearby Raivata garden. Under an Ashok tree, he took off all his ornaments and the royal dress, and pulled out five fistfuls of hair. He became an ascetic along with one thousand people. Shri Krishna, deeply touched by this incident, blessed his cousin and wished him success in his mission.

Monk Nemkumär went to mount Girnar. He stood motionless, intensely meditating, trying to find the cause of all unhappiness. He realized that ignorance of the true nature of the Self led to wrong perception, and consequent wrong actions resulted in all sorts of misery and pain. He therefore dwelled deep into the Self.

After spending fifty-four days in deep spiritual meditation at Mount Girnar, Neminäth destroyed all his Ghäti Karmas which were obscuring the true nature and power of the soul. He attained Keval-jnän and became an omniscient. He established the four-fold religious order (This Chaturvidha Sangha is known as a Tirtha) and became the twenty-second Tirthankar of the Jain religion. Thereafter, he lived a long life preaching the path of liberation to the common people.

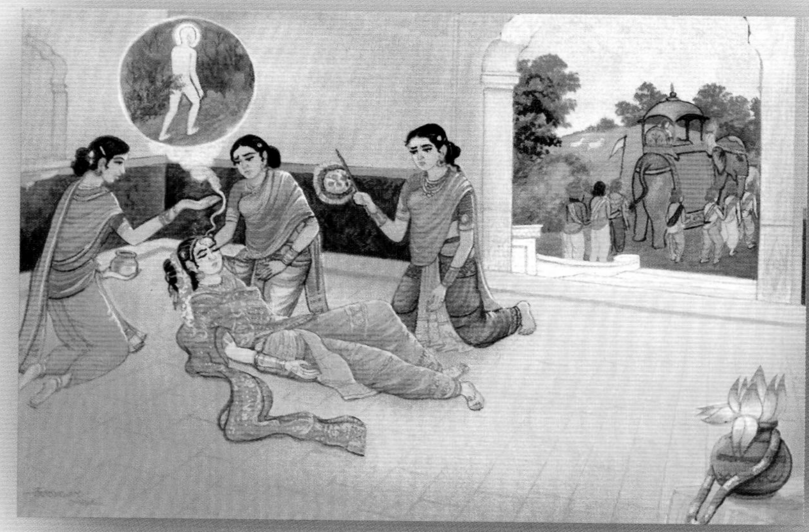

Friends consoling Princess Räjul

At the time when Neminäth decided to renounce his worldly life, Räjul was being adorned by her girl friends. She was eagerly waiting for the arrival of her Nemkumär as the bridegroom. Then they heard the news that Nemkumär had turned back. No one could understand his decision. Räjul was in utter grief. A calamity had overtaken her all of a sudden! Her friends tried to console her in that hour of crisis. Some of them started cursing Nemkumär for putting their beloved friend in such a miserable condition. Some advised her to forget the unpredictable Nemkumär and look for another suitable match. In her heart, Räjul had accepted Nemkumär as her husband. She could not even think of any other person taking his place. She did not like anyone cursing Nemkumär or speaking poorly of him.

She had some spiritual orientation also. When she came to know of the real cause of his renouncement, she was able to overcome her grief. She realized that Nemkumär had left for a commendable purpose. She could appreciate his mission. She thought that the best way for her was to follow his footsteps. She absorbed herself in religious practices.

When Räjul heard that Neminäth had become an omniscient she went to the Samavasaran along with many of her friends and took Dikshä. She absorbed herself in meditation and penance and spent the rest of her life as the head of the nuns' order. In the end, after destroying all her Karmas she attained liberation.

Bhagawän Neminäth's life is a good example of compassion towards animals. The killing and torture of animals on his account rekindled his passion for the search for complete freedom from misery. Räjul was a noble princess who appreciated Nemkumär's search for truth and happily followed him.

05 Bhagawän Pärshvanäth

About 3000 years ago, King Ashvasen was ruling over the Kingdom of Väränasi also known as Banäras, in India. The city is situated on the banks of the holy River Gangä. He was a benevolent and a popular ruler and lived peacefully with his Queen, Vämädevi. On the 10th day of the dark half of the month of Märgashirsh (which usually falls in December) Queen Vämädevi gave birth to a son. Once, during her pregnancy, she had observed a snake passing by. The passing of that snake made quite an impression on her. In memory of that incident, her newborn son was named Pärshva-kumär, because in the Sanskrit language 'Pärshva' means 'near by or in the vicinity'.

Pärshva grew up in the midst of wealth and happiness and became a very attractive young man known for his courtesy, bravery, and valor. His reputation was well-known in all the kingdoms and many kings were eager to have their daughters marry him. Prince Pärshva-kumär was married to Prabhävati, a princess from a neighboring kingdom. The wedding ceremony was performed with much splendor and Pärshva-kumär enjoyed a blissful married life with Prabhävati.

At that time, there was a mendicant named Kamath. During his childhood he had lost his parents and was raised as an orphan. Disgusted with his miserable life he had become a mendicant. As a mendicant, he had no material possessions and lived on the charity of others. He practiced severe penance and performed rituals called Panchägni (five fires). He came to Väränasi to perform the Panchägni (five fires) ritual. Many people were impressed by his ritual and penance and therefore worshipped him.

Pärshva-kumär reciting Namaskär Mantra to the half-burnt snake

When Pärshva-kumär heard about Kamath's ritual, he realized the violence towards living beings involved in a fire. He came to Kamath and tried to dissuade him from lighting the sacrificial fire. Kamath denied that any life was at stake because of his ritual. However, by extra sensory perception, Pärshva-kumär sensed a snake trapped inside one of the burning logs. He asked his men to remove the log and chop it carefully. To everyone's surprise, a half-burnt snake came out of the burning piece of wood. Pärshva-kumär recited the Namaskär-mantra for the benefit of the dying snake. The snake was so badly burnt that he soon died. After death, the snake was reborn as Dharanendra, the king of gods of the Nag kumärs (gods or angels that look like snakes) in heaven.

Instead of feeling remorse or pity for the snake, Kamath was very annoyed by the interference of Pärshva-kumär but was powerless at that time. He resolved to seek revenge. Kamath began observing an even more severe penance and at the end of his life he was reborn in heaven as Meghamäli, the god of rain.

Observing the miseries that living beings had to experience in their worldly life, Pärshva-kumär developed a high degree of detachment towards worldly possessions and relationships. At the age of 30, he renounced all his possessions and his family and became a monk. Later on, he was known as Pärshvanäth. He spent most of his time meditating in search of the ultimate truth. Once, while he was in meditation, Meghamäli saw him from heaven. He recalled how Pärshva-kumär had interfered in his ritual and penance in an earlier life and saw his chance for revenge.

Using his supernatural powers, he brought forth all kinds of fierce and harmful animals such as elephants, lions, leopards, and snakes to attack monk Pärshvanäth. However Pärshvanäth, immersed in deep meditation, remained peaceful and untouched. Then Meghamäli tried a new tactic and brought forth heavy rains. The rainwater touched the feet of Pärshvanäth and started accumulating. The water rose up to his knees, then to his waist, and in no time it reached his neck.

Dharanendra noticed that Pärshvanäth, his benefactor was going to drown in the rising floodwater. Immediately Dharanendra descended and placed a quick growing lotus flower below Pärshvanäth's feet so that he could float on the water. Then he spread his fangs over the head and sides of Pärshvanäth in order to protect him from the pouring rain. Dharanendra then severely reprimanded Meghamäli for his wretched act and asked him to stop the rain. All of Meghamäli's efforts to harass Pärshvanäth were in vain. He was disappointed and realized that he was unnecessarily creating trouble for the graceful, merciful Lord. He withdrew all his supernatural powers and fell at Pärshvanäth's feet with a sense of deep remorse. He

Meghamäli causing distress to Bhagawän Pärshvanäth

sincerely begged the Lord to forgive him for his evil acts.

During that period of distress, Pärshvanäth had been deep in meditation. He had not been aware of Meghamäli's attacks or Dharanendra's protection. Pärshvanäth had developed perfect equanimity. He did not have any special affection for Dharanendra for the protection he had extended or hatred for Meghamäli for the distress he had caused. Developing a higher purity of consciousness, he ultimately attained omniscience on the 84th day of his renunciation. That was the 4th day of the dark half of the month of Falgun (that usually falls in April).

Dharanendra protecting Bhagawän Pärshvanäth

Pärshvanäth then began preaching true religion. He reinstated the Tirtha or religious four-fold order and became the 23rd Tirthankar of the Jain religion. He attracted many followers. He had ten Ganadhars, the principal disciples of Tirthankars. His parents and his wife Prabhävati renounced the world and became his disciples as well. Thereafter, he lived long enough to spread true religion and attain nirvana at the age of 100 at Sametshikhar. This hill is located in the state of Bihar and is the most famous place of pilgrimage for Jains.

Pärshva-kumär demonstrated a very keen sense of non-violence and detachment from all material possessions and from relationships with people. These are the qualities essential for attaining self-realization. He showed us that one should be detached and impartial regardless of whether a person is our well-wisher or enemy. We may not always know and understand the reason why a person behaves in a strange way towards us for it may be because of our Karmas from a past life.

Part II
Ganadhars and Ächäryas

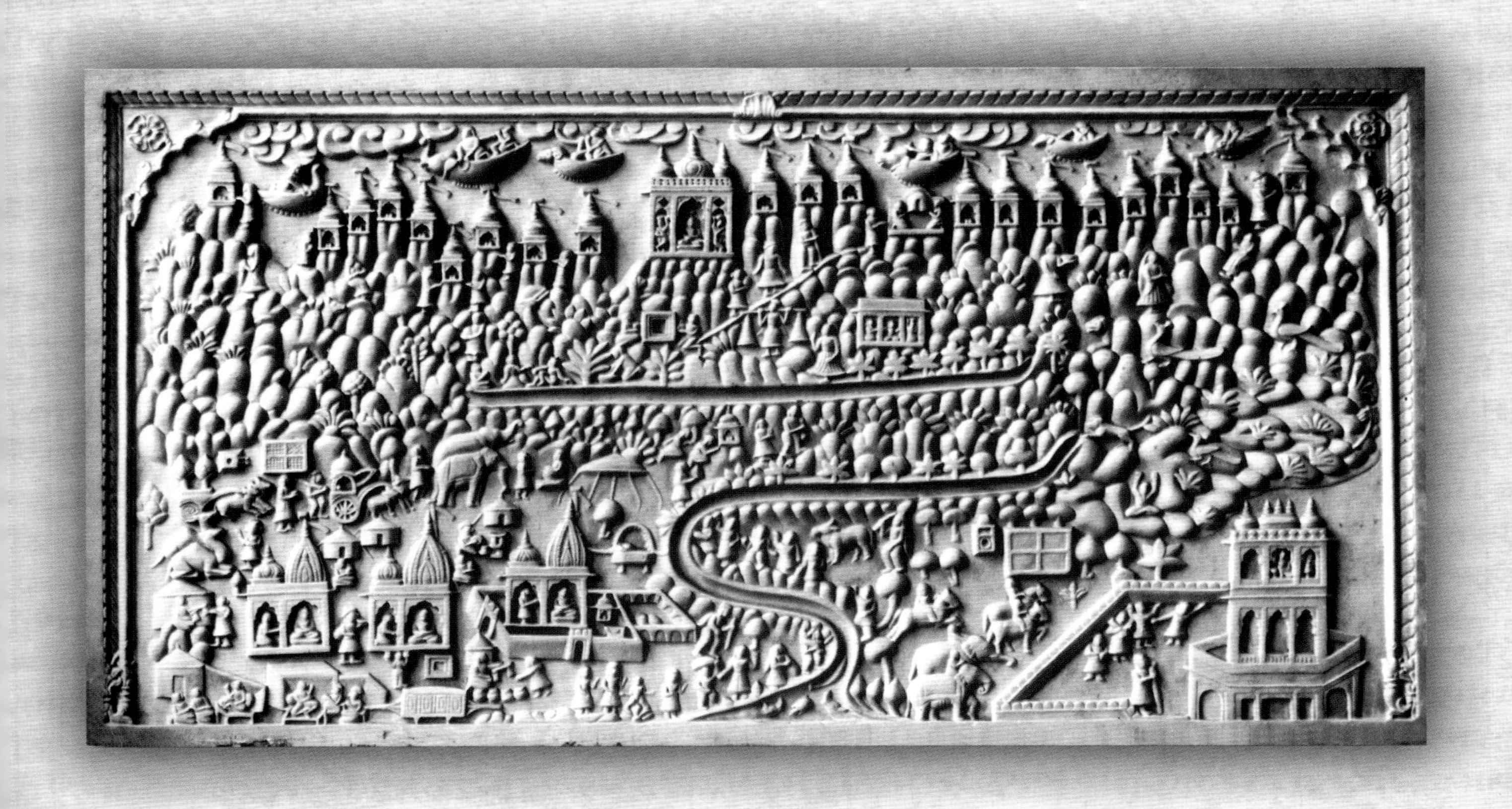

"I do not favor Mahävir,
nor am I prejudiced against Kapil.
I would accept anyone's statement
provided I find it true on the scale of logic"

- Lokatva Nirnaya of Haribhadra

06 Ganadhar Gautam-swämi

In 607 B.C., in the village of Gobar, state of Magadha, India, lived a Brahmin couple named Vasubhuti and Prithvi Gautam. They had three sons, Indrabhuti, Agnibhuti and Väyubhuti. All three sons were well versed in the Hindu scriptures (Vedas) and were experts in the performance of Hindu rituals. They were great scholars at an early age. Each one of them had 500 disciples.

Somil's Yajna

Once in the nearby city of Apäpä, a Brahmin named Somil had organized a sacrificial ceremony or Yajna at his home. Forty-four hundred Brahmins gathered for the occasion and eleven popular scholars were among them. Indrabhuti Gautam stood out among the eleven as a shining star. He was the head priest conducting the ceremony.

The whole town was excited by this event in which they were going to sacrifice sheep and goats. As he was about to begin his ritual everyone noticed many celestial beings from heaven descending towards the sacrificial site. Indrabhuti internally rejoiced thinking that this would make the sacrificial ceremony the most famous in history. He told the people, "Look at the sky. Even the celestial beings are descending from heaven to bless us." Everyone eagerly looked up at the sky.

To everyone's surprise, the celestial beings did not stop at their site. They continued past their site and headed towards the nearby Mahäsen forest. Indrabhuti learned that the celestial beings were going to pay homage to Bhagawän Mahävir who had just attained Keval-jnän and was about to deliver his first sermon in the language of the common people called Ardha Mägadhi - Präkrit.

He was furious that the celestial beings did not pay their respect to his sacrificial rite. He angrily thought to himself, "Who is Mahävir? He does not even use the rich Sanskrit language to deliver his sermon, but speaks the common people's language of Ardha Mägadhi." He decided to debate with Mahävir in order to prove to the celestial beings that he was more knowledgeable than Mahävir. So he left with his 500 disciples to debate with Mahävir.

Mahävir welcomed Indrabhuti by his name even though they had never met before. At first, Indrabhuti was caught off guard, but then he thought, "Why should Mahävir not know my name? I am Indrabhuti Gautam, the famous scholar."

Also Bhagawän Mahävir's omniscience (unbounded knowledge) allowed him to know all of Indrabhuti's thoughts. Mahävir realized that Indrabhuti had come to debate with him. He also realized that Indrabhuti had doubts about the existence of the soul or Ätmä.

Mahävir said, "Indrabhuti, do you doubt the existence of soul?" Then he explained that the soul exists and it is eternal. He provided proper interpretation of the Hindu scriptures (Vedas) and convinced Indrabhuti that the soul does exist. Indrabhuti was shocked and surprised that Mahävir knew his doubts about the existence of the soul and the proper interpretation of his scriptures. He felt awakened, refreshed, and realized how incomplete his knowledge had been. He became Mahävir's first and chief disciple. Indrabhuti was fifty years old at the time and from then on he was called Gautam-swämi, as he came from the Gautam family.

Meanwhile, Somil and the other ten scholars were waiting to greet the expected winner of the debate, Indrabhuti Gautam. However, they were stunned to learn that Indrabhuti had become a disciple of Mahävir. The other ten Brahmin scholars, with their disciples, immediately set out to debate with Mahävir and became his disciples too. Dejected and abandoned, Somil cancelled the ceremony and set all the animals free. These eleven learned scholars were the main disciples of Lord Mahävir and they are called the eleven Ganadhars.

Bhagawän Mahävir answering queries raised by Pundits and teachers

Änand Shrävak's Clairvoyance Knowledge

Gautam-swämi was living his life as a Jain monk observing all the austerities and following the five great vows. Once, while returning from Gochari (getting food or alms), he learned that many people were going to pay homage to Änand Shrävak (a Jain layman). He also learned that Änand Shrävak had attained clairvoyance knowledge known as Avadhi-jnän by performing severe penance and austerities. Since Änand Shrävak was one of Mahävir's followers, Gautam-swämi decided to visit him.

When Änand saw Gautam-swämi approaching his house, he was very happy. Though weak, due to his austerities, he got up and welcomed Gautam-swämi. He inquired about Änand's health and asked about his special knowledge. With respect, Änand replied to Gautam-swämi, "Reverend Guru, I have attained Avadhi-jnän. With this knowledge I can see as high as the first heaven and as low as the first hell." Gautam-swämi explained to Änand, "A layman (Shrävak) can attain Avadhi-jnän, but not to this magnitude. You need to do Präyashchitta (atonement) for believing you can do this." Änand was puzzled. He knew that he was correct but his guru questioned his truthfulness and told him to repent for it. He therefore politely asked Gautam-swämi, "Does one need to repent for speaking the truth?" Gautam-swämi was equally puzzled and replied, "No one has to repent for speaking the truth." Thinking that he would confirm this with Bhagawän Mahävir, Gautam-swämi left Änand.

Gautam-swämi returned to Bhagawän Mahävir and asked about Änand's clairvoyance knowledge. Mahävir replied, "Gautam, Änand was telling the truth. He can see as high as the first heaven and as low as the first hell. Rarely can a layman attain such a level of Avadhi-jnän. You should repent for your mistake of doubting him." Mahävir valued truth and would never conceal the mistake of his disciple to protect his own image. Gautam-swämi set aside his alms and immediately returned to Änand and asked for his forgiveness.

Offering food to 1500 Hermits

On another occasion, Gautam-swämi went to a temple on Mount Ashtäpad to pay homage to the 24 Tirthankars. The mountain was very difficult to climb. At the foothill of the mountain fifteen hundred hermits were trying to climb the mountain but they were not successful. They saw Gautam-swämi complete this difficult journey and were very impressed. They decided to be his disciples. Gautam-swämi preached to them about true religion and the correct ways of penance and accepted them as his disciples. All fifteen hundred hermits became Jain monks. Gautam-swämi realized that they were hungry and offered them Kheer (rice pudding) from a small Pätra (bowl).

They began to wonder how Gautam-swämi would feed all of them. Gautam-swämi requested all the hermits to sit down. Since he possessed a special power called Akshin-mahänasi Labdhi (non-diminishing power), he served everyone Kheer from his small bowl. While serving Kheer he kept his thumb in it to invoke the power. To everyone's surprise, they all were well-served from this small Pätra.

Gautam-swämi's Keval-jnän

As time passed, all the disciples of Gautam-swämi attained Keval-jnän, the ultimate knowledge. However Gautam-swämi was still unable to attain it. He was worried that he may not attain Keval-jnän in this life. One day Gautam-swämi asked Lord Mahävir, "Ten other scholars joined me on the day that I accepted Dikshä and all eleven of us became your disciples. Nine of them have attained Keval-jnän. All my disciples have attained Keval-jnän. Why am I so unlucky that I am not able to attain Keval-jnän?" Lord Mahävir replied, "Gautam, it is because you have too much affection for me. In order to attain Keval-jnän you must overcome all types of attachment, including attachment to your beloved Guru. Until you give up your attachment towards me, it will not be possible for you to attain Keval-jnän."

On the day that Lord Mahävir was going to attain Nirvana (liberation), he sent Gautam-swämi to a nearby village to preach to a man named Devsharma. On his way back, Gautam-swämi learned that Lord Mahävir had attained Nirvana. Gautam-swämi lapsed into a state of shock and sorrow, "Lord Mahävir knew that this was his last day on Earth. Why did he send me away?" Gautam-swämi could not stop his tears. He also thought, "I could not attain Keval-jnän while Mahävir was alive. Now there is no hope of attaining Keval-jnän because he is gone forever." However within a few minutes he realized his error and began thinking, "No one can live forever. No relationship is permanent. Why am I so attached to Lord Mahävir?" He contemplated that he was wrong and gave up his attachment towards Mahävir. During this deep thinking, he destroyed his Ghäti Karmas and immediately attained Keval-jnän at the age of eighty. He attained Nirvana at the age of ninety-two in 515 B.C.

Lord Mahävir attained nirvana on the last day of the Jain and Hindu calendar known as Deepävali day and Gautam-swämi attained Keval-jnän on the first day of the New Year.

Gautam-swämi attaining omniscience

Gautam-swämi was a Brahmin by birth and a very well learned Pundit. When he met Bhagawän Mahävir and realized that Mahävir was far more knowledgeable and spiritually advanced than him, he let go of his ego and became his disciple. Gautam-swämi repented for his mistake to Änand Shrävak, a layperson, and asked for his forgiveness. He was the first and main disciple of Bhagawän Mahävir. However, it took him a long time to attain omniscience even though many other disciples had attained it much earlier than he. This was due to his attachment for Mahävir-swämi. In Jainism, attachment to any individual is considered a passion. To attain omniscience, one must get rid of all passions. When Gautam-swämi realized this and became detached, he attained Keval-jnän.

07 Ganadhar Sudharmä-swämi

Ganadhars are the immediate disciples of a Tirthankar. Bhagawän Mahävir had eleven Ganadhars. All of Bhagawän Mahävir's monks were divided into 11 groups and each group was placed under a Ganadhar. When Bhagawän Mahävir attained Nirvana, only two of the eleven Ganadhars were still living, the first Ganadhar, Gautam-swämi and the fifth Ganadhar, Sudharmä-swämi.

Gautam-swämi attained Keval-jnän the day after Mahävir's Nirvana. It is a Jain tradition that a Kevali monk or nun remains in a meditative state for the rest of his/her life and does not provide a leadership role to other monks. Hence, Sudharmä-swämi became the leader of all of the ascetics and the entire Jain community after Lord Mahävir's Nirvana.

Sudharmä-swämi was the son of a learned Brahmin named Dhammil and his wife Bhaddilä. They lived in a village called Kollag, now known as Kollua in the state of Bihar, India. Dhammil and Bhaddilä both longed for a child. Bhaddilä worshipped goddess Saraswati (goddess of knowledge) faithfully. It is said that the goddess, pleased by her devotion, blessed Bhaddilä by promising her a highly accomplished son. Soon after that, Bhaddilä became pregnant, and in due course gave birth to a son named Sudharmä. He was born in 607 BC, and was 8 years older than Lord Mahävir.

Sudharmä grew up under the loving care of his parents. At an appropriate age, he went to a well-known Äshram (boarding school), where he studied the Vedas, Upanishads, and all other Hindu (Brahmanical) literature. He was a diligent scholar. By the time he returned from school, he was famous and well respected as a learned Brahmin Pundit. He then started his own school, which became a center of great learning. Over 500 pupils from all over the country came to study under his tutelage.

At that time in Päväpuri (also known as Apäpä), a city in Bihar, there lived a prosperous Brahmin named Somil. He had organized a great sacrificial Yajna. He invited all the well-known scholars of the time to the event. Indrabhuti Gautam, who was the most learned Brahmin of that time, was the presiding priest. His equally learned brothers, Agnibhuti and Väyubhuti, attended along with seven other well-known Pundits. Sudharmä was also invited.

At the appointed time, the sacrificial ceremony began. At that time, the attendees noticed many celestial chariots descending towards the earth. Indrabhuti and the other priests were jubilant that they could persuade the celestial beings to descend and accept their respects. However, they were soon disappointed to see that the chariots passed over their ceremonial site and continued towards the nearby Mahäsen forest.

The celestial beings had actually come to pay their respects to Bhagawän Mahävir who had arrived at Päväpuri at the same time. After attaining Keval-jnän, Bhagawän Mahävir was going to deliver his first sermon and establish the Jain order.

Indrabhuti was outraged that the celestial beings did not pay their respect to his sacrificial rite. He decided to debate with Mahävir in order to prove to the celestial beings that he was more knowledgeable than Mahävir. So he left with his 500 followers to debate with Mahävir. He went to the place where Lord Mahävir was giving the sermon. As he approached, the Lord welcomed him saying, "Welcome Indrabhuti Gautam." Indrabhuti was surprised. Then Bhagawän Mahävir addressed his doubts pertaining to the existence of the soul. After the explanation Indrabhuti and his 500 followers became the disciples of Mahävir.

Ganadhar Sudharmä-swämi

Since Indrabhuti did not come back, his brothers Agnibhuti, Väyubhuti, and another Pundit, Vyakta, went to Bhagawän Mahävir one after another. Bhagawän Mahävir welcomed them, and addressed their doubts pertaining to different aspects of the soul and Karma. All of them were satisfied with Lord Mahävir's knowledge and they, along with their own disciples, became disciples of Lord Mahävir.

Then it was Sudharmä's turn. Sudharmä believed that every living being would reincarnate into its own species. In other words, human beings would be reborn only as human beings. His theory was based on the analogy of plant life. An apple tree, for instance, would produce the seeds from which only other apple trees could grow. Bhagawän Mahävir welcomed him too. He calmly and patiently explained to Sudharmä that human beings could be reincarnated as humans or heavenly beings or even as animals depending upon their Karma. He addressed all of Sudharmä's doubts and explained to him the theory of Karma. Sudharmä saw the wisdom of Bhagawän Mahävir's words and was convinced with the explanation and he too became a disciple of Bhagawän Mahävir. As a Ganadhar of Bhagawän Mahävir, he came to be known as Sudharmä-swämi. Sudharmä brought with him his five hundred disciples.

He was then followed by the remaining six Brahmin scholars. All eleven pundits became the Ganadhars of Bhagawän Mahävir. Dejected and abandoned, Somil cancelled the sacrificial ceremony and set all the animals free.

This happened when Mahävir was 42 years old and had just attained omniscience. Mahävir lived for another 30 years. During that period he continued to travel to different parts of the country in order to spread the message of compassion and explain the path of liberation. During those discourses, Sudharmä-swämi always sat in front of him and carefully listened to what Bhagawän Mahävir had to say. This enabled him to compose Mahävir's teachings in the form of Jain scriptures known as Ägams.

After Mahävir's Nirvana in 527 BC, the leadership of the Jain order was left to Sudharmä-swämi. During the next 12 years that he remained at the helm, he efficiently managed the Jain order set up by Bhagawän Mahävir and spread his message far and wide.

Shvetämbar tradition believes that during the period of his stewardship, Sudharmä-swämi organized Bhagawän Mahävir's teachings into 12 scriptures, known as the 12 Anga Ägams. These original scriptures (Ägams), are collectively known as Dvädashängi. Dvädasha means 12, and Anga means limb (part). Many of the Ägams are composed in the form of questions asked by Jambu Swämi (Sudharmä-swämi's disciple) and replies given by Sudharmä Swämi indicating Bhagawän Mahävir's reply. Sudharmä-swämi attained omniscience in 515 BC and attained Nirvana in 507 BC at the age of 100. After attaining omniscience, the religious order was entrusted to his principal disciple Jambu Swämi.

Jainism has deep roots and we practice it based on the scriptures that have passed down for many generations. The scriptures called Ägams, compiled by the Ganadhars, comprise of the preachings of Mahävir-swämi. We do not have the benefit of the presence of such great monks as Gautam-swämi and Sudharmä-swämi in this era, but we do have the benefit of learning those principles from the scriptures. Thus, we should take advantage of the scriptures that have passed down through many generations.

08 Kevali Jambuswämi

In the city of Räjgrihi, there lived a wealthy merchant named Rushabhadatt. His wife, Dhärini, gave birth to a very handsome son named Jambu in 542 BC. He grew up into a very bright and intelligent young man, well liked by everyone. When he became older, many families were eager to have their daughters marry him. It was a normal practice in those days for a man to have more than one wife. His parents selected 8 girls from reputed families and Jambu was duly engaged to all of them. It was a joyous time for all.

One day, Ganadhar Sudharmä-swämi came to Räjgrihi to deliver a sermon. Jambu went to the assembly to hear the sermon. The sermon encouraged him to develop a very high sense of detachment towards worldly objects and family members. He decided to renounce his worldly life. Jambu's parents were dismayed to hear about him renouncing the world at such a young age. The parents of the eight girls who were engaged to Jambu were also very worried that now no one else would marry their daughters because of their engagement to Jambu.

They all tried to convince Jambu to relinquish his plan of becoming a monk. They indicated the rigors of ascetic life that would pose a challenge for him. They tried to convince him that he did not fully understand what he was sacrificing for this ascetic life. His parents reminded him of his obligations towards them and his futures wives. They advised him to live a comfortable family life. Jambu listened to them with patience but he remained firm in his decision.

The parents made one last effort to persuade him. They thought that Jambu would change his mind after the wedding. Therefore, they requested him to get married before they gave their blessing for his renunciation. Jambu agreed to get married with one condition that he would become an ascetic the day after his marriage. His parents agreed to this condition since they thought that he would fall in love with the girls once he was married, and would give up the idea of renouncing the world.

The wedding took place on a grand scale. Jambu's parents and those of the girls contested with one another in showing their prosperity. No effort was spared in making the wedding a memorable ceremony. Highly distinguished guests graced the occasion. The jewelry and other precious gifts that were showered upon the newly weds were the envy of everyone. Räjgrihi had rarely witnessed such pomp and splendor. Every one congratulated Jambu for marrying such beautiful and glamorous wives and wished him perfect happiness. Jambu spent that night in an elegantly decorated bedroom with his wives.

Jambu was unaffected by the glamour nor did the beauty of those lovely girls overcome him. He had firmly decided to renounce the world the next day and wanted to make use of the night to orient his wives for spiritual pursuit. He started explaining the temporary and transitory nature of life and the miserable nature of worldly relationships.

While Jambu was engrossed in a discussion with his wives, a famous burglar named Prabhav and his 500 followers entered the palace of Jambu. Prabhav was once the prince of Vindhya, a neighboring city of Räjgrihi. He and his parents had a disagreement and he had left the palace. He became a thief and a leader of 500 devout followers. Prabhav had acquired special skills that were very useful in his current profession. With his special skills, he could put anyone into a deep sleep and could break any lock.

Prabhav had come to town to steal the fabulous treasures accumulated on the occasion of Jambu's wedding. He used his skills to put every one into a deep sleep and to open the locks. He and his 500 followers quickly entered the palace to steal the wedding treasures. As Prabhav approached Jambu's suite he heard Jambu talking to his wives. Somehow, his power did not affect Jambu and his wives. He came closer to the door in an effort to listen closely. To his utter astonishment, Jambu was talking about renunciation and the misery associated with worldly life. His words were so powerful that Prabhav became interested and continued listening.

He pondered over the irony of how hard he worked to steal wealth, while the owner was planning to renounce everything. Jambu continued to preach to his wives and Prabhav listened to the conversation quietly. His men finished stealing from the rest of the palace and urged Prabhav to finish the job of stealing the jewelry located in Jambu's bedroom so they could leave before the guards discovered them.

By now, Prabhav had lost his desire for wealth, had developed a disdain for the life of a burglar and was ready to change. He told his followers that he had decided to give up burglary. They were free to go on their own. However, they said that they would not go anywhere without him. If he gave up robbing and stealing, they would also give it up.

Jambu Kumär preaching to his wives

When Jambu finished the religious discussion with his wives, all his wives were ready to renounce the world. At this time, Prabhav came inside and said that he had come there to steal but had decided to renounce everything after listening to Jambu's talk with his wives. He and his 500 followers made up their mind to become Jambu's disciples.

In the morning, the citizens of Räjgrihi awoke to some surprising news. Jambu, his eight wives, the famous thief Prabhav, and his 500 followers were ready to renounce their worldly lives that day. Jambu's parents were saddened and disappointed that their wish did not materialize. They quickly realized the importance of Jambu's message and decided to join him also. Hearing the news and understanding the message, the parents of the eight brides also renounced the world. A spectacular procession followed Jambu on his way to see Sudharmä-swämi. Jambu bowed to Sudharmä-swämi and became his disciple and in turn, Prabhav and his colleagues became Jambu's disciples.

Jambuswämi, as he became known henceforth, studied the entire teachings of Lord Mahävir. Most of the original Jain scriptures (12 Anga Ägams) are composed in the form of dialogues between Sudharmä-swämi and Jambuswämi. Jambuswämi became the head of the religious order when Sudharmä-swämi attained omniscience. He remained the head of the Jain order for 44 years and then he attained omniscience (Keval-jnän). He was the last omniscient (Kevali) of the current time cycle. He attained Nirvana at the age of 80.

Jambuswämi firmly believed in renouncing the worldly life from the moment he listened to the sermon of Sudharmä-swämi. In fact, his thoughts were so convincing that it ultimately led hundreds of others to follow him in their pursuit of liberation through the disciplined life of an ascetic. He realized that material happiness and enjoyment of physical beauty is all superficial and temporary. Also noteworthy is the burglar's decision to change his life from that of immorality to that of purity. The key is to focus on purifying the soul and helping others to do the same.

09 Ächärya Sthulibhadra

The kingdom of Magadha, in the state of Bihar, possessed a long and rich history. During Mahävir's time it was ruled by King Shrenik of the Shishunäg dynasty. This dynasty ended with the death of Shrenik's great grandson Udayi. Magadha then passed into the hands of the Nanda dynasty, where Dhanänand succeeded nine generations of his family's rule. This was around 300 BC or about 200 years after Lord Mahävir's nirvana.

Dhanänand was far from being a just and noble ruler as he was very greedy. He had heard a legend about some hidden treasure that belonged to one of his predecessors and was desperate to get his hands on it. Unfortunately, he had no idea where this treasure was hidden. However, he knew that his old Prime Minister Shaktäl, who had served his father, had knowledge of the treasure's whereabouts. Dhanänand tried everything he could to locate the treasure, but Shaktäl refused to provide any information about the whereabouts of this treasure. The king then forced him to retire and the administration was entrusted to the other ministers.

Shaktäl was a wise, knowledgeable, and highly respected person in the kingdom. Many scholars and high ranking officials admired him and were eager to consult him on important matters. However, they avoided communicating with him because they feared that the king would not approve of this.

Shaktäl had seven daughters and two sons, Sthulibhadra and Shriyäk. Sthulibhadra was smart, brilliant, and handsome, but not very ambitious. In Patliputra, the capital city of Magadha, there lived a beautiful young dancer named Koshä. From a very young age, Sthulibhadra would watch her perform. They fell in love with each other. His family disapproved of the relationship. However, Sthulibhadra was deeply in

Kumär Sthulibhadra enjoying Koshä's dance

love. He left home at the young age of 18 and started living with Koshä. He was infatuated with Koshä and abandoned all interest in his career and other family members. King Dhanänand intended to appoint him to a high position in the court but Sthulibhadra declined the offer. The king therefore appointed his younger brother, Shriyäk, to the position.

As time passed, things began to look grim for Dhanänand's reign. The citizens of Magadha witnessed major political upheavals and turmoil. People felt dissatisfied with the current regime and looked for the end of the Nanda dynasty. King Dhanänand felt insecure and was suspicious of all his ministers and advisors including Shriyäk and his father Shaktäl. Shaktäl also knew that the king was very suspicious of him. Hence, he was worried about the political future of his younger son.

Shaktäl decided to sacrifice his life in order to provide proof of Shriyäk's loyalty to the king. He requested his son, Shriyäk, to kill him in the presence of the king and other ministers. This way the king would have proof that Shriyäk was a very loyal minister. He explained to Shriyäk, that prior to the execution he would swallow some poison. This way Shriyäk would not truly (morally and religiously) be responsible for his father's death. And the king would feel that Shriyäk was very loyal to him because he killed his own father. Thus, Shaktäl arranged to die at the hands of his own son in order to prove his son's loyalty.

When Sthulibhadra learned about that tragic event, he was taken aback. By that time, he had spent 12 years with Koshä and had never cared for anyone else. His father's death was an eye opener. He started reflecting on his past. "Twelve long years of my youthful life! What did I get during this long period?" He realized that he had not acquired anything that would endure. The tragic end of his father brought home the reality that all life comes to an end. "Is there no way to escape death?" He asked himself, "What is the nature of life after all? Who am I and what is my mission in life?"

Delving deep into these questions, he realized that the body and all worldly aspects are transitory, and physical pleasures do not lead to lasting happiness. He looked at his image in the mirror and noticed the unmistakable marks of a lustful life. He also realized that he was wasting his youth. He decided to search for lasting happiness. He left Koshä and went straight to Ächärya Sambhutivijay who was the sixth successor to Lord Mahävir. Surrendering himself to the Ächärya, he said that he was sick of his lustful lifestyle and wanted to do something worthwhile with his life. Here was a young man of thirty who seemed to have lost the vigor of youth. The lustful life he had led had taken a toll on his body; but the brightness inherited from his illustrious father still glowed on his face. Seeing Sthulibhadra's determined and humble state, the learned Ächärya saw in him a great future for the religious order and accepted him as his pupil.

Sthulibhadra did not lose much time to adjust to the new pattern of his life. The ambition that he had missed in his youth emerged in the man. He was keen to make up for lost years and devoted all his energy to spiritual upliftment. He worked diligently and in no time gained the confidence of his guru. His life as a monk was exemplary. He had successfully overcome his senses of attachment and lustfulness, and gained control over his inner enemies. It was time for his faith to be tested.

The monsoon season was approaching and the monks had to settle in one place during the rainy season. Sthulibhadra and three other monks (Sädhus) who had attained a high level of equanimity wanted to test their faith and determination by spending the monsoon time (4 months as per Indian climate) under the most adverse conditions. Each one chose the most adverse conditions for themselves. One of them requested permission from his Ächärya to stay at the entrance of a lion's den; another wanted to spend the time near a snake's hole; the third wanted to spend the 4 months on top of an open well. The Ächärya knew that they were capable of withstanding these hardships and permitted them. Sthulibhadra humbly requested that he would like to spend the monsoon in the picture gallery of the residence of Koshä. The Ächärya knew how difficult this test would be for Sthulibhadra. However, the Ächärya also knew Sthulibhadra's determination and felt that spiritually he would not progress any further without passing this test. Therefore, he permitted Sthulibhadra to spend the monsoon at Koshä's house.

Sthulibhadra approached Koshä and asked her permission to stay in the picture gallery during the monsoon season. Koshä was surprised to see him. He had left her in such an ambivalent state that she had not been sure if she would ever see him again. She was missing him and was happy to see him again. However she did not know the true purpose of his return. They both had their goals for the monsoon season. Koshä endeavored to win him back into her life. She used all her seductive skills and felt that having him live in her picture gallery was to her advantage. Sthulibhadra's goal was to overcome the strong temptation of Koshä's beauty. Who would win? Sthulibhadra's strong faith and determination served him well during this test. He focused his mind on spiritual meditation. He spent his time meditating on the transitory nature of life and the need to break away from the cycle of birth and death. Ultimately, Koshä realized the wastefulness of her life and became his disciple. Sthulibhadra emerged spiritually stronger from this experience.

At the end of the monsoon, all the monks returned and described their experience. The first three monks described their success and they were congratulated. When Sthulibhadra reported the success of his test, the Ächärya rose from his seat in all praise and hailed Sthulibhadra for performing a formidable task. The other monks became jealous. Why was Sthulibhadra's feat so much more impressive than theirs? After all, they had endured physical hardships while he had spent the monsoon in comfort and security. The Ächärya explained that it was an impossible feat for anyone else. The first monk boasted that he could easily accomplish the same task the following monsoon. The Ächärya tried to dissuade him from his intent because it was beyond his capability. The monk wanting to prove his spiritual strength to the Ächärya, persisted and was reluctantly given permission for the next monsoon season.

The next monsoon the monk went to Koshä's place. The immodest pictures in the gallery were enough to excite him. When he saw glamorous Koshä, his remaining resistance melted away and he begged for her love. After seeing the pious life of Sthulibhadra, Koshä had learned the value of an ascetic life. In order to teach the monk a lesson, she agreed to love him only if he gave her a diamond-studded garment from Nepal, a town 250 miles north of Patliputra. The monk was so infatuated that he left immediately for Nepal, forgetting that monks were not supposed to travel during the monsoon. With considerable difficulty, he procured the garment and returned to Patliputra confident of receiving Koshä's love. Koshä accepted the beautiful garment, wiped her feet on it and threw it away in the trash. He was stunned. He asked her, "Are you crazy, Koshä? Why are you throwing away the precious gift that I have brought for you with so much difficulty?" Koshä replied, 'Why are you throwing away the precious life of monkhood that you have acquired with so much effort?' The humbled monk realized his foolishness and returned to his Ächärya to report on his miserable failure. There was immense respect for Sthulibhadra from that day onwards.

Sthulibhadra played a major role in later years to preserve the oldest Jain scriptures known as the twelve Anga Ägams and the fourteen Purvas. Jain history indicates that Ächärya Bhadrabähu was the last monk who had complete knowledge of all the Jain scriptures. Ächärya Bhadrabähu succeeded Ächärya Sambhutivijay as head of the religious order. Both Ächärya Sambhutivijay and Ächärya Bhadrabähu were the disciples of Ächärya Yashobhadra.

In those days, the Jain scriptures were memorized and passed on orally from guru to disciple. They were not documented in any form. Under the leadership of Ächärya Bhadrabähu, Sthulibhadra thoroughly studied eleven of the twelve Anga Ägams.

An extended famine prevented Sthulibhadra from studying the twelfth Anga Ägam known as Drashtiväda, containing the fourteen Purvas. During the famine Ächärya Bhadrabähu-swämi migrated south with 12,000 disciples. Ächärya Sthulibhadra succeeded him as the leader of the monks who stayed behind in Pataliputra. The hardships of the famine made it difficult for the monks to observe their code of conduct properly. In addition, many of the monks' memories failed them and many parts of the Anga Ägams were forgotten.

The famine lasted for twelve years. After the famine, Sthulibhadra decided to recompile the Jain scriptures. A convention was held in Patliputra under the leadership of Sthulibhadra. Eleven of the twelve Anga Ägams were orally recompiled at the convention. None of the monks at the convention could remember the twelfth Anga Ägam and its 14 Purvas. Only Ächärya Bhadrabähu swämi had this knowledge but he had left southern India and was now in the mountains of Nepal to practice a special penance and meditation. The Jain Sangha requested Sthulibhadra and some other learned monks to go to Ächärya

Bhadrabähu-swämi and learn the twelfth Ägam. Several monks undertook this long journey but only Sthulibhadra reached Nepal. He began to learn the twelfth Anga Ägam and its 14 Purvas under Ächärya Bhadrabähu.

Once Sthulibhadra's sisters who were nuns, decided to visit him in Nepal. At this time, Sthulibhadra had completed 10 of the 14 Purvas. He wanted to impress them with the miraculous power he had acquired from learning the 10 Purvas and knowledge from the twelfth Ägam. He transformed his body into a lion. When his sisters entered the cave, they found a lion instead of their brother. Fearful of what may have happened to him they went directly to Bhadrabähu-swämi. Ächärya Bhadrabähu realized what had happened and asked the sisters to go back to the cave again. This time Sthulibhadra had resumed his original form and the sisters were joyful to see him alive and well.

However, Bhadrabähu-swämi was disappointed that Sthulibhadra had misused his special power for such a trivial purpose. He felt that Sthulibhadra was not mature enough in his spiritual progress and therefore refused to teach him the remaining four Purvas. A chastised Sthulibhadra tried to persuade him to reconsider but Bhadrabähu-swämi was firm. It was only when the Jain Sangha requested Ächärya Bhadrabähu to reconsider his decision that Sthulibhadra was allowed to learn the remaining four Purvas. But Ächärya Bhadrabähu attached two conditions for Sthulibhadra:

- He would not teach Sthulibhadra the meaning of the last four Purvas
- Sthulibhadra could not teach these four Purvas to any other monk

Sthulibhadra agreed and learned the remaining four Purvas.

Since Jain scriptures were not written down and Ächärya Sthulibhadra had made significant effort to save them after the famine, his name stands very high in the history of Jainism. Even today, his name is recited next to Lord Mahävir and Gautam-swämi by the Shvetämbar tradition.

It is never too late to set high goals in life, and with determination there is no adversity too difficult to overcome. Though he was 30 at the time, and had wasted 12 years of his life, Sthulibhadra still renounced the world and successfully pursued an austere spiritual life. With resolve he also conquered his biggest inner enemy, desire, by returning to the place where his desire had previously got the best of him. Ultimately, he became a famous Jain saint whose name is still repeated in prayers for his great religious work.

10 Ächärya Kunda-kunda

मंगलं भगवान वीरो, मंगलं गौतमो गणि ।

मंगलं कुन्दकुन्दार्यो, जैन धर्मोस्तु मंगलं ॥

mangalam bhagaväna viro, mangalam gautamo gani |

mangalam kundakundäryo, jaina dharmostu mangalam ||

Bhagawän Mahävir is auspicious; Ganadhar Gautam Swämi is auspicious;

Ächärya Kunda-kunda is auspicious; Jain religion is auspicious.

The great spiritual saint Kunda-Kundächärya occupies the highest place in the tradition of Jain Ächäryas. He is remembered immediately after Bhagawän Mahävir and the preceptor Gautam Ganadhar as an auspicious blessing. Everyday, Digambar Jains recite the couplet with the three adorable reverentially before starting the study of religious texts. Jain monks feel honored in being included in the tradition of Kunda-Kundächärya.

In the southern state of Tamilnadu in India, atop a hill known as Ponnur Malai, on a large stone under a certain Champä tree, pilgrims may stumble upon an engraved pair of footprints (Charan). These footprints are symbolic of a thinker who, nearly two thousand years ago, composed some of the most influential philosophical books. Generations of scholars can remember the exact day of their first encounter with this thinker's spiritual masterpiece, the Samay-sär.

Ächärya Kunda-kunda is one of the most famous Jain Ächäryas. He is a great organizer of the highly complex concepts of Jain philosophy. He is the celebrated author of five renowned books:

- Samay-sär (Treatise on the True Self)
- Pravachan-sär (Treatise of Preaching)
- Niyama-sär (Treatise on Rules of Conduct)
- Panchästikäya (Treatise on Five Universal Substances)
- Ashta-pähud (Eight Steps), a collection of eight texts

All his works are written in an ancient dialect known as Saurseni Präkrit which is similar to Ardha-mägadhi Präkrit. The organizing of Jain ideas into certain relationships and structures, taken for granted in recent centuries, was a product of his genius. So extraordinary was this idea that many other books written in this style by his pupils and other Jain scholars are popularly ascribed to him. In the Digambar tradition, he is praised immediately after Lord Mahävir and the preceptor Gautam-swämi in the auspicious blessing

(Mangalächaran) prayer. Jains of the Digambar tradition dub their tradition Kunda-kunda Anvaya (the order of Kunda-kunda). However, scholars of all sects study his books with deep veneration.

He was born around the beginning of the first century AD in Southern India in a place named Konda-konda. Kunda-kunda belonged to an ancient order called the Nandi Sangha, wherein most monks assumed names ending in "Nandi". His official name after becoming a Jain monk was Padma-nandi, but he is better known by the place of his origin. Kunda-kunda mentions that he was a descendant of Bhadrabähu-swämi, the last Shruta Kevali Ächärya who possessed complete knowledge of the twelve Anga Ägams including the 14 Purvas.

Punya Shrävak Kathä Kosha mentions that in his previous life Kunda-kunda was a cow herder who had found and preserved ancient texts and was blessed by a wandering monk. Ächärya Kunda Kunda's intense learning and moral character attracted royal disciples such as King Shiva Kumar. The story of Kunda-kunda is also surrounded by a legend – it is even said that he could walk on air!

Ächärya Kund-kunda

Kunda Kunda's influence extends far beyond Jainism. India has always been a land where philosophical debates are a standard feature of intellectual life. The concise and systematized aphorisms he brought to Jain literature were unparallel. Kunda-kunda's creativity allowed him to utilize existing literary structures to explain Jainism's most advanced scientific principles such as atomic structure, cosmic dimensions, the cosmic ethers, and psychology. His treatises rivaled any other writing to date. Hindu and Buddhist thinkers were challenged to respond to his explications of Jain philosophy and conduct. Kunda-kunda elevated the level of scholarship and debate in India's overall philosophical discourse.

Out of enthusiastic respect, Ächärya Kunda-kunda has been called "Light of this Dark Age". Several commentaries on his Samay-sär have been written in Sanskrit and in modern languages. In recent centuries, the Samay-sär has greatly moved leaders and scholars like Banärasi Das, Tarana Swämi, Shrimad Räjchandra and Gurudev Shri Kanji Swämi.

11 Ächärya Haribhadra-suri

During the sixth century A.D., there lived a learned Brahmin named Haribhadra. He was highly intelligent and proficient in the philosophy of all religions. Among his many talents was the ability to determine the point of his opponent's argument very fast. During that time it was common for scholars to travel and engage others in debate to increase their wealth of knowledge. Therefore, Haribhadra traveled and met many brilliant scholars. He engaged them in debate and succeeded in defeating them all. Other scholars found it difficult to win any discussion with him since his talent allowed him to dominate all conversations. It was not long before he earned a reputation as a formidable opponent. Predictably, scholars avoided entering into a discussion with him.

When no one came forward to counter him, he concluded that he had no rival in the entire country. He felt confident of his ability to comprehend anything that anyone would like to discuss. He therefore issued a public challenge that if any one could present a topic that he could not understand he would readily become his/her pupil.

One day as he was walking through the village he came across a royal elephant. The elephant was very angry and completely out of control. His keeper was trying his best to bring him under control but the elephant was not responding to his efforts. The elephant was running directly towards Haribhadra and he was in grave danger of being trampled. Haribhadra had to find shelter quickly. He frantically looked around for a safe place and saw a Jain temple. He rushed towards it and entered just in time to avoid being crushed by the charging elephant. He paused inside to regain his breath and then looked around the temple in disrespect. Haribhadra had no regard for Jainism. Because of his prejudice he remained ignorant of Jain philosophy. Brahmins were usually staunch Shaiväites (followers of Lord Shiva in Hinduism) and looked down upon those going to Jain temples.

As he entered the temple he saw the white marble idol of Lord Mahävir facing him. Instead of seeing the graceful compassion flowing from the eyes of the Tirthankar's idol, Haribhadra only noticed that the stomach of the idol did not epitomize the slim body of an austere saint. He surmised that Jain Tirthankars must have enjoyed sweet foods. He therefore made the following remarks:

"Vapurevatavächashte Spashtam Mishtänn-Bhojitämit"

"Your stomach clearly indicates that you must enjoy eating sweet foods"

When the elephant left the area, Haribhadra stepped outside the temple. On his way back, he passed the Upäshray of Jain nuns (Sädhvis). He heard the following verse that was recited by a Sädhvi named Yäkini Mahattarä:

Chakkidugam Haripanagam Panagam Chakki Ya Kesavo Chakki

Kesav Chakki Kesav Du Chakki Kesi Ya Chakki Ya

Mahattarä was explaining the order in which the Chakravartis (sovereign emperors) and Väsudevs were born in the current Avasarpini time cycle. Jain philosophy believes in time cycles of very long durations occurring one after another. One half of a cycle is called Utsarpini, or the ascending order marked with continuing improvements, and the other half is called Avasarpini, or the descending order marked with continuing deterioration. Tradition also holds that 24 Tirthankars, 12 Chakravartis (sovereign emperors), 9 Väsudevs or Näräyans, 9 Prativäsudev or Prati-Näräyans (enemies of Väsudevs) and 9 Balräms are born in every Utsarpini as well as in every Avasarpini time cycle.

Haribhadra-suri accepting monkhood under Ächärya Jinbhatta

As a student, Haribhadra had studied some Jain philosophy. However, his understanding was very shallow and so he could not comprehend the meaning of what Sädhvi Mahattarä was reciting. Haribhadra was at loss about what to do. Finally, he had stumbled upon a subject he did not dominate; however, to seek more knowledge required him to become a pupil of Jain Sädhvi Mahattarä. He was perplexed. Despite his arrogance, Haribhadra was also a man of his word. Without further hesitation, he presented himself to the Jain nun Mahattarä, explained his pledge, and requested her to accept him as a pupil. Mahattarä explained that Jain nuns could not have males as pupils. She advised Haribhadra to go to her Guru Jinabhatta-suri who could explain the meaning of the verse and he could become a pupil of her Guru. Accordingly, Haribhadra went to Ächärya Jinabhatta-suri who explained the verse in the proper perspective.

The Ächärya's explanation of the verse induced Haribhadra to learn more about Jainism. He requested the Ächärya to accept him as a pupil. Jinabhatta-suri agreed to accept him only if he got the consent of his family and other close relatives. Haribhadra knew that it would be an ordeal to get their consent to study Jainism. Indeed, his family opposed his decision. His father challenged him, "But you have studied so much to become a Brahmin scholar. Why would you want to give that up now?" His relatives, who had been so proud of his reputation cried, "But you are the best debater. Who will you be now?" Haribhadra persevered in the face of this resistance. He explained to them that his knowledge would remain incomplete without gaining knowledge of Jainism in detail. For that purpose as well as for adhering to his decision, it was necessary for him to be a Jain monk. He ultimately succeeded in gaining the consent of all his family members. Thereupon, he renounced his worldly life and became a disciple of Ächärya Jinabhatta-suri.

He diligently studied Jain scriptures and other sacred books. His intelligence and perception soon allowed him to achieve mastery of Jain scriptures. The study of the Ägams showed him the depth of Jain philosophy in seeking the truth. Once he mastered all the relevant Jain literature and when his Guru Jinabhatta-suri was thoroughly convinced about his true faith, he decided to bestow upon Haribhadra the title of Ächärya. Now Haribhadra became Ächärya Haribhadra-suri. As an Ächärya he managed the Jain order very capably and efficiently. By virtue of his knowledge and intelligence he attracted many people to Jainism. Many of them also renounced worldly life and became his disciples. Jainism gained a newfound popularity under his stewardship.

Amongst his many pupils there were two pupils named Hans and Paramhans, who were his sister's sons. They were very intelligent, and Haribhadra-suri had high expectations of them. Once, Hans and Paramhans requested him to allow them to go to a well-known Buddhist monastery in order to study the weak points of Buddhism. Then, they could defeat the Buddhist monks in debate. Haribhadra-suri did not approve. Hans and Paramhans persisted and ultimately they secured his permission. They went to the monastery disguised as Buddhist monks. Unfortunately, their secret was quickly revealed. They decided to leave the monastery in disguise. The Buddhist people were chasing them which ultimately resulted in the loss of their lives.

When Haribhadra-suri learned about the tragic fate of his nephews, he was furious and vowed to punish the Buddhist monks for their cruelty. He challenged them to a debate in the royal court with the stipulation that whoever lost would be put to death. Haribhadra-suri's violent reaction to his nephews' deaths saddened Guru Jinabhatta-suri and Sädhvi Mahattarä. Haribhadra-suri won the debate but Sädhvi Mahattarä convinced him to abandon the idea of killing. Haribhadra-suri also realized that his undue attachment for Hans and Paramhans had led him to indulge in such a violent attitude. He therefore begged for atonement. Guru Jinabhatta-suri advised him to compose verses that would enlighten people to the right faith. This was another major turning point in his life.

Haribhadra-suri was a prolific writer. He wrote 1444 religious books covering many aspects of Jainism. Unfortunately only about 170 of his books are presently available.

The commentaries on Dash Vaikälika-sutra, Tattvärtha-sutra, Pancha-sutra, and Ävashyaka-sutra are among his well-known compositions. Moreover, he wrote Lalit-vistarä, Dharma Sangrahani, Upadeshapad, Shodashtaks, Dharmabindu, and Anekänta Jayapatäkä. He was probably the first Jain scholar to write on Yoga. Yogabindu, Yoga-vinshikä, Yoga-shatak and Yogadrashti Samuchchaya are his compositions on Yoga. He will always be remembered for his valuable contribution to Jain literature.

The entire life of Haribhadra-suri depicts his keen desire for learning. Even though he was an established Brahmin scholar, he was humble enough to learn from a simple Jain Sädhvi. This is a great lesson in humility. One should not let pride come in the way of acquiring knowledge. Jain Ägams describe the essence of Jainism in a logical and convincing manner. A deep understanding of the Ägams will lead one to practice the principles of Jainism with more discipline and faith. The various compositions of Haribhadra-suri are very precious and help us gain a better understanding of this very complex but well-defined and logical religion.

12 Ächärya Hemchandra

Ächärya Hemchandra was born in 1088 A.D. in the Modha Vanik (merchant) caste in the town of Dhandhuka, sixty miles from the city of Amdavad in Gujarat State, India. His parents were Chachadev and Pähini. While Pähini was pregnant, she had a beautiful dream. She narrated her dream to Jain Ächärya Devasuri who was in Dhandhuka at that time. The Ächärya predicted that Pähini would give birth to a son who would make great progress in the areas of spiritual knowledge, conduct, and logic. When her son was born, she named him Chängdev.

Various incidences from Ächärya Hemchandra and King Kumärpäl's life

The next time Ächärya Devasuri was in Dhandhuka, he saw Pähini carrying her son. He said to Pähini, "Let me take care of this brilliant son. He has the potential of being a great spiritual leader." Pähini refused to relinquish her son to him. The Ächärya persisted and reminded her that her son would become a famous monk and would glorify the Jain order. He requested her to sacrifice self-interest and love for the child for the good of the people at large. Finally, Pähini surrendered and gave her son to the Ächärya. He initiated Chängdev into Jain monkhood and renamed him Somchandra.

Somchandra was very intelligent and very quickly mastered various philosophies, logic, scriptures, Nyäya, grammar, and more. Simultaneously, he cultivated excellent virtues like forbearance, tolerance, holiness, simplicity, discipline, chastity, and generosity. Somchandra was incomparable in administration and efficiency. Ächärya Devasuri made Somchandra an Ächärya when he was only twenty-one years old and called him Hemchandra Ächärya.

The fame of Hemchandra's knowledge gradually spread everywhere. A higher and noble form of culture was established due to the efforts of Hemchandra and the cooperation of King Siddharäj of Gujarat. When King Siddharäj died, Kumärpäl succeeded him. King Kumärpäl and Hemchandra Ächärya were to enjoy a life long relation of teacher and disciple. The seeds of this spiritual relation had already been sown. Ächärya Hemchandra had predicted seven years back that Kumärpäl would become king and he had once saved the future king's life. Kumärpäl considered Hemchandra his spiritual teacher (Guru) and benefactor and gave him exceptional honor. Kumärpäl sought Hemchandra's advice in shaping his kingdom, and in a very short time Gujarat became a center of non-violence, learning, and good culture.

In his efforts, Hemchandra did not think of the development of his own career but always of the welfare of all citizens. However, some Brahmins were very jealous of Hemchandra Ächärya's influence over the king and they tried to disgrace him and Jainism. They approached King Kumärpäl and criticized, "Hemchandra Ächärya is a very egoistic person and has no respect for Hindu Gods." King Kumärpäl was not ready to accept these accusations against his spiritual guru. To prove their point, the Brahmins requested King Kumärpäl to invite the Ächärya to the temple of Lord Shiva. They sought to humiliate the Ächärya in front of the king since they believed that he would not go to the temple and bow down to Lord Shiva. When Hemchandra Ächärya appeared, King Kumärpäl said, "We will go to the temple of Lord Shiva." He accepted the offer without any hesitation. The Brahmins, barely able to conceal their joy, were delighted that their plan was working. To the surprise of the Brahmins, Hemchandra Ächärya bowed down in front of Lord Shiva and said,

"Bhavbijänkura jananä Rägädyähä Kshaymupagata Yasya;

Brahmä Vä Vishnurvä Haro Jino Vä Namastasmai."

"I am bowing down to that God who has destroyed passions like attachment (Räga) and aversions (Dvesha) which are the cause of worldly life whether he is Brahma, Vishnu, Shiva, or Jin."

By this modest act, Hemchandra Ächärya proved his noble attitude in his willingness to respect other faiths and pray to the virtues of other deities. This generous attitude is inherent in Jain philosophy. Jainism does not hold itself superior to other religions, but as peacefully coexisting with them. Under Ächärya Hemchandra's influence King Kumärpäl accepted Jainism. He prohibited violence and the killing of any animals in his kingdom. King Kumärpäl made many laws that nurtured Jain religion. Vegetarianism was found not only in Jains but also in all the people of Gujarat.

Ächärya Hemchandra composed several literary works consisting of many verses. He was the first to put non-violence on a political platform and he was the architect of the greatness and unification of Gujarat. In the field of metaphysics, he was a Yogi. His work Yoga-shästra, a treatise on yoga, is very famous. People called him 'Kali-käl Sarvajna' meaning 'all knower in the present era of darkness'. He died in 1173 A.D. at the age of eighty-four. Jain culture still shines bright in Gujarat due to the influence of the literary works contributed by the great Ächärya Hemchandra.

Mother Pähini's sacrifice of her love for her son is very praiseworthy. It is a great gift to the Jain religion. It is because of Hemchandra Ächärya that Kumärpäl accepted Jainism and became a Jain. It is because of this that Jainism and vegetarianism flourish in Gujarat. Hemchandra Ächärya's contribution of numerous literary masterpieces is a treasure for us. Only by studying these books, we can pay tribute to him.

Part III
Stories Preceding Bhagawän Mahävir

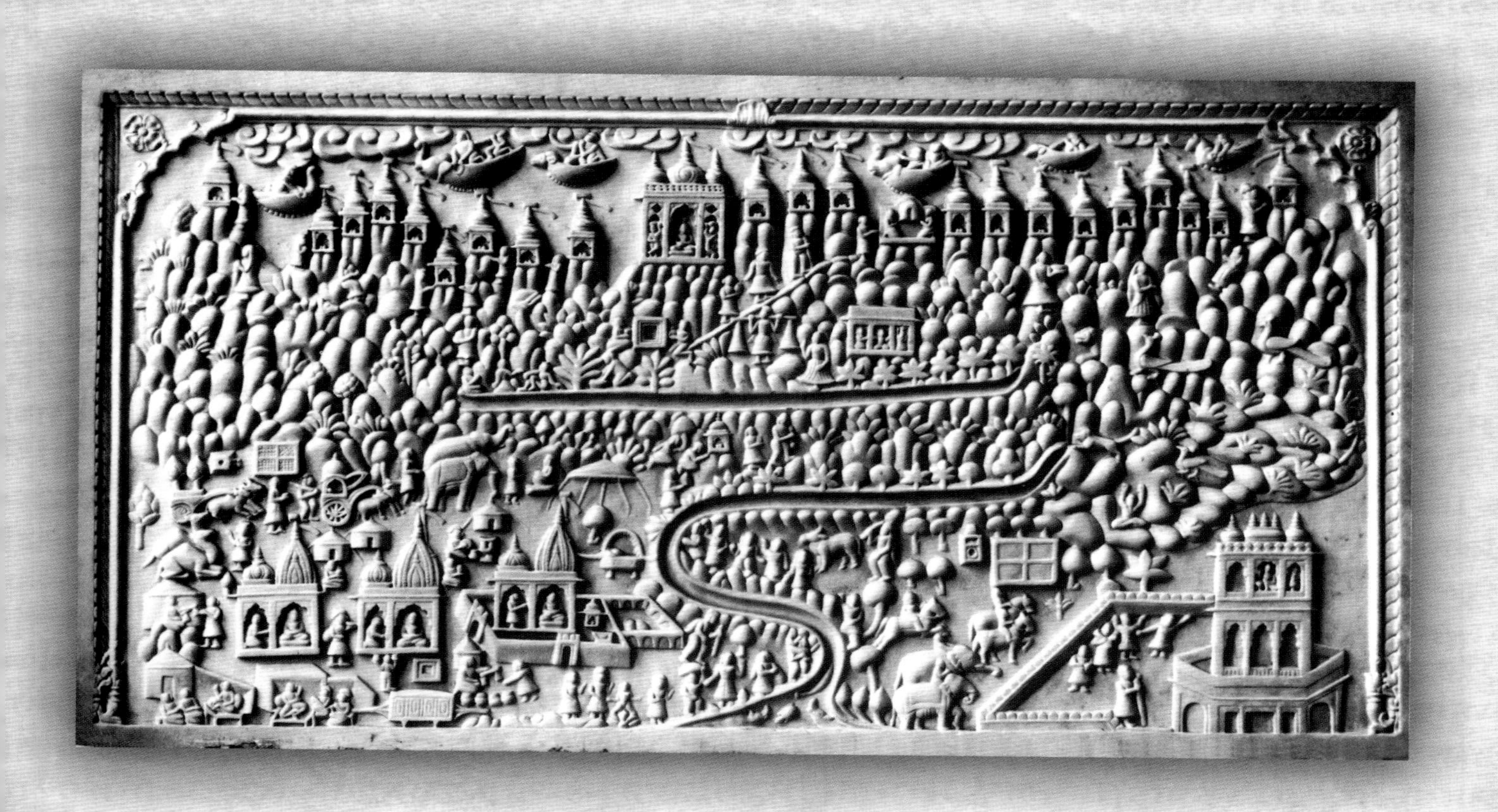

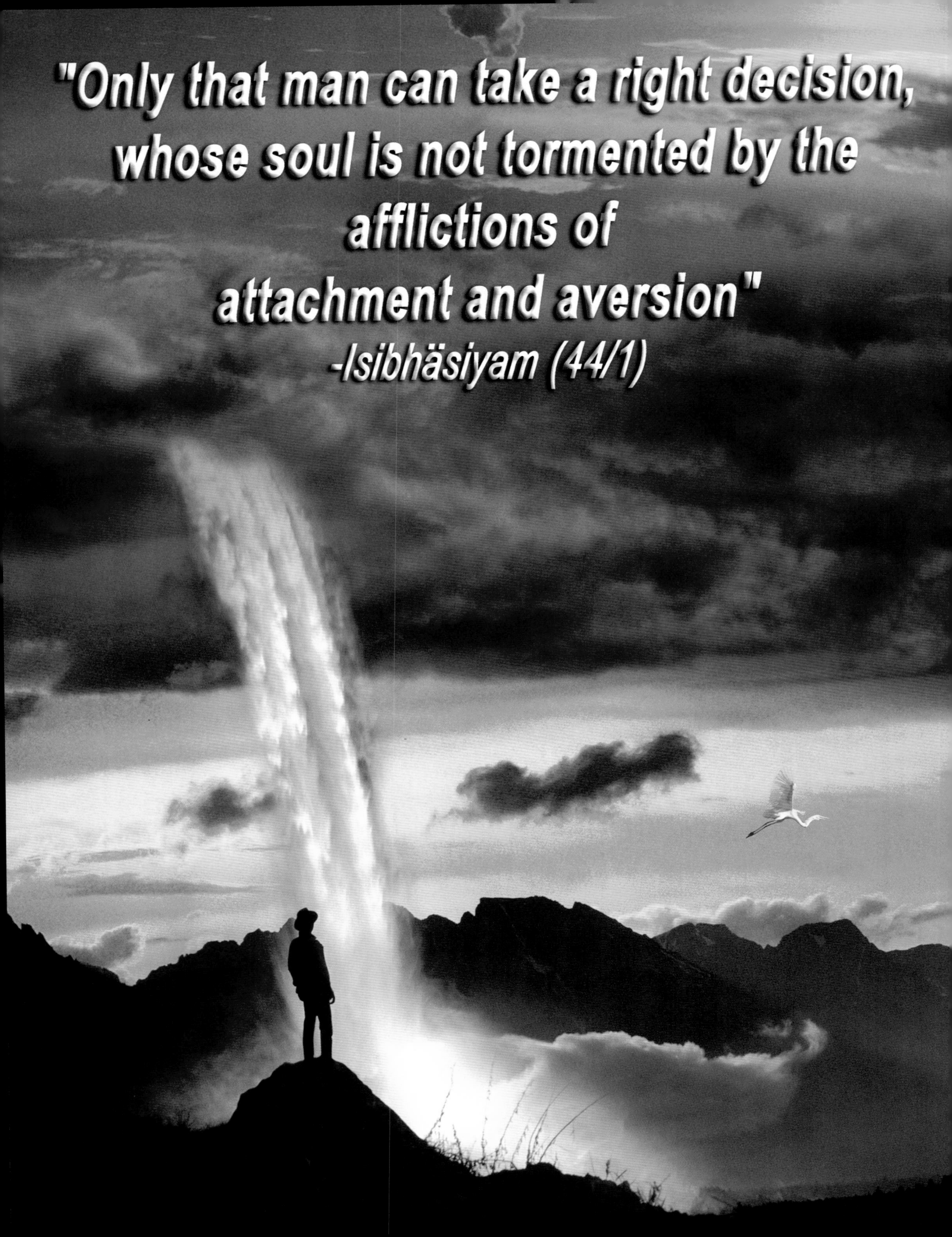
"Only that man can take a right decision,
whose soul is not tormented by the
afflictions of
attachment and aversion"
-Isibhäsiyam (44/1)

13 Bharat and Bähubali

Lord Rishabhadev or Ädinäth was known as king Rishabhadev before his renunciation of worldly life. He had two wives, Sumangalä and Sunandä. By Sumangalä, he had 99 sons, of whom Bharat was the eldest and the best known, and one daughter named Brähmi. By the second wife, Sunandä, he had one son named Bähubali and a daughter named Sundari. All of them were given proper training in different arts and crafts. Bharat became a great warrior and a politician. He was tall, well built, and strong and hence was called Bähubali. In Sanskrit, Bähu means arm and Bali means mighty. Brähmi attained a very high level of literary proficiency. She developed the first known script known as Brähmi script. Sundari was very proficient in mathematics. After Lord Rishabhadev attained omniscience, both girls renounced their worldly lives and became his disciples.

As a king, Rishabhadev had the responsibility of a large kingdom. At the time of his renunciation, he handed over the city of Vinitä, also known as Ayodhyä, to Bharat; and the city of Taxshilä (Potanpur according to Digambar scriptures) to Bähubali. To the remaining 98 sons he gave different parts of his vast kingdom.

Bharat quickly established control over Vinita. He was an ambitious ruler and intended to become emperor of the entire nation. For this purpose, he organized a strong army and started developing different types of fighting equipment. He also possessed a miraculous wheel called Chakraratna (Chakra means wheel and Ratna means precious jewel) that would never miss its target. Then he embarked upon his journey of conquest. In those days, there was hardly anyone who could withstand his well-equipped army. He easily conquered all the regions around Vinitä. Then he turned his attention towards his 98 brothers and asked them to acknowledge his superiority. They all turned to Lord Rishabhadev to ask for advice. Bhagawän explained about conquering their inner enemies (passions) and not external enemies. He also advised them on attaining liberation, a "True Kingdom". They all realized the futility of fighting with their elder brother; so they surrendered their territories to him, renounced worldly life and became disciples of Lord Rishabhadev.

Now only Bähubali remained and he would not surrender. He had a different vision. He was conscious of his right to rule the kingdom handed over to him by his father. Moreover he had the will and capacity to fight any invader. Therefore, when he received Bharat's request to accept a subordinate status, he refused and began preparations to fight. Both brothers were strong and war between the two was sure to result in large-scale bloodshed. Therefore, counselors on both sides tried to dissuade their masters from resorting to war but neither of them would give up his ground. War seemed inevitable and both the brothers brought their armies face to face on the battlefield. Everyone shuddered at the prospect of the heavy casualties that would result from the imminent war.

The counselors made one last effort. They explained to their masters that the main point of contention was to determine which brother was superior. Instead of assembling a large-scale war for that purpose, a fight between the two brothers would just as easily settle the issue and would avert unnecessary bloodshed. Both brothers thought this was an excellent idea and immediately agreed. The plan was to engage in a straight duel and the victor of the duel would be acknowledged the leader.

Bharat and Bähubali both agreed to the rules. The day of the duel arrived. Bharat tried to beat Bähubali by using his various permissible weapons. All his attempts to defeat Bähubali failed. Bharat contemplated how unbearable and shameful his defeat would be. His ambition to rule the entire world was also at stake if he did not defeat his brother. He grew desperate and ignored the rules of the duel by unleashing his miracle wheel, the Chakraratna, at Bähubali. Bharat forgot one important characteristic of the miracle weapon that it would not harm any blood relatives of the bearer. Therefore the wheel returned to Bharat and Bähubali remained unharmed. Bähubali became enraged by Bharat's violation of the rules of the duel. He thought of smashing the elder brother with his mighty fist. As he raised his hand for that purpose, the onlookers trembled at the thought of Bharat's imminent death.

Incidences in the lives of King Bharat and King Bähubali

Just as he was about to unleash his wrath, a flash of insight came to him. "What am I doing?" thought Bähubali. "Have I gone mad? Am I going to kill my elder brother for the sake of some worldly possessions that my revered father willingly abandoned and which my other brothers have given up?" He shuddered at the prospect of the imminent death of Bharat. At that moment he changed his mind. He saw the evil in killing a brother he respected. Instead of lowering his hand to hit his brother, he used it to pull out his hair (as the monks do during Dikshä - renunciation ceremony) as a symbol of giving up everything and of renouncing the worldly life.

But Bähubali had not lost his pride and ego. He realized that if he went to his father and stated his intention of renouncing the world he would be required to bow down and be subservient to his 98 younger brothers who were senior to him in monkhood. This was unacceptable to him. Instead, Bähubali decided to seek enlightenment on his own and started meditating on the very spot that he stood. He became so immersed in his meditation that he lost track of time and could not remember how long he had stood there. He stood in that very spot for so long that creepers began to grow around his feet.

A year passed with Bähubali standing in that posture of meditation. Yet, he did not gain enlightenment. How could he gain it without shedding his ego? At last, Lord Rishabhadev sent Brähmi and Sundari to bring him to the right path. They came to the place where Bähubali was meditating. Seeing their mighty brother standing like a rock, they calmly told him, "You cannot get enlightenment while sitting on an

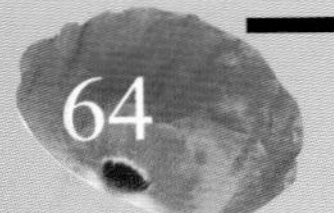

elephant. You need to get off the elephant." As their familiar voices reached Bähubali's ears, he opened his eyes in amazement and looked around but did not find himself on an elephant. He then realized that the elephant they were referring to was his ego. He immediately dissolved his ego and decided to go to Lord Rishabhadev and was ready to bow to his 98 brothers.

During his long penance, he had overcome all other defiling passions except ego which still remained between him and enlightenment. Now his ego was dissolved and humbleness prevailed in its place. Therefore, as he took the first step towards the Lord he achieved full enlightenment and became omniscient. Bähubali became the first person who attained liberation in this era as per Digambar sect. However, Shvetämbar tradition indicates that Rishabhadev's mother Marudevi attained liberation first in this era.

In memory of this event, a gigantic 57-foot upright statue of Bähubali stands on the hill of Vindhyagiri at Shravanbelgola, near Bangalore in southern India. It is made out of a single rock of granite and was erected about 1000 years ago. Pilgrims and visitors marvel that the statue, even under the open sky, stands spotless today.

Idol of Bähubali at Shravanbelgola

Meanwhile, Bharat had become the undisputed emperor or Chakravarti of the world. He was the first Chakravarti of the current time cycle of Avasarpini Ärä. He ruled equitably and in the interest of all. People were happy during his administration. India was recognized as Bhäratvarsha. He himself was happy in every respect and ruled for a very long time.

One day a ring slipped off his finger while he was in his dressing room. He noticed that the finger looked rather odd without the ring. His curiosity overtook him and he removed all his rings and saw that his fingers were no longer beautiful. Then he took off his crown and other ornaments that used to decorate his body and looked in the mirror. He noticed that he did not look as handsome as he used to look.

This set off a train of thoughts. 'I consider myself handsome and strong but this entire look is merely due to the ornaments which do not belong to the body. The body itself is made up of blood and bones. Then why am I so attached to my body?' He thought further. 'My body will not last forever and will decompose sooner or later. At that stage, I will have to leave everything behind. The only everlasting entity is the soul.' He thus realized that nothing in the world, including his body, really belonged to him. He came to a major decision. "Why not do away with my attachment of all the temporary things and instead focus on something that lasts forever like my father did?" Thus, he developed an acute detachment for the worldly life. As per Shvetämbar tradition, this reflection led to the rise of true enlightenment from within and as a result he attained omniscience or Keval-jnän in that very room as a lay person. Digambar tradition indicates that after an acute detachment of worldly life, he renounced that life and became a monk. Immediately after becoming monk, he attained Keval-jnän. At the end of his life he attained liberation.

The focus of this great story is on ego and self-realization. Ego and pride build negative Karma and lead one to destructive behavior as detailed in the story. Ego also causes anger and leads one to irrational behavior. Ego and superficial pride must be overcome on the path to enlightenment and omniscience. We should all strive for cultivating humility, one of the fundamental principles of Jainism.

14 King Megharath

One day Indra, the king of heavenly gods, praised the bravery and mercifulness of King Megharath on Earth during an assembly of demigods. He mentioned that king Megharath would not hesitate to give up his own life to protect those who came to him for shelter. Two demigods doubted Indra's statement. So Indra asked them to go to Earth and see for themselves. Since they could not appear on Earth in their heavenly forms; one of them decided to take the form of a pigeon, and the other took the form of a hawk.

Down on Earth, King Megharath was sitting in his court surrounded by his courtiers. Suddenly a pigeon flew in through an open window and started circling the hall. To the king's surprise, it landed on his lap. It was shaking uncontrollably. The king realized that the pigeon was shaking with fear and had flown into the palace to seek refuge.

At that very instant, a hawk flew into the king's court. He said to the king, "This pigeon is my food. Let me have him." The king was dumbfounded to hear a bird talk! However, he replied, "It is true that this pigeon is your food, but now it is under my shelter. I will not give you this pigeon, but I can give you some other food."

He ordered his servants to bring a basket of fruits and vegetables. However, the hawk said, "I am not a human being, and I am not a vegetarian. I need meat (flesh) for my food."

King Megharath offering his own flesh to save a bird's life

The king said, "Let me give you my own flesh instead of this pigeon's flesh." Upon hearing this, one of the courtiers said, "Your Majesty, why should you give your own flesh? Let's get the meat from a butcher."

King Megharath offering his own life to save a bird's life

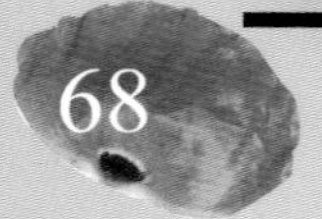

The king replied, "No, because the butcher will have to kill another animal in order to supply us the meat. This pigeon has sought refuge and it is my duty to protect it. At the same time, it is also my duty to see that no one else is harmed in the process. Therefore, I will give my own flesh to the hawk."

With these words, he took out his knife and cut off a piece of flesh from his thigh and offered that to the hawk. The whole court was stunned. However, the hawk said to the king, "Oh king, I want the same amount of flesh as the pigeon."

Therefore, a weighing scale was brought to the court. The king put the pigeon on one side and a piece of his own flesh on the other. The king kept adding more and more of his flesh on the scale, but it was not enough. Finally, the king got ready to put his whole body on the scale. The court was stunned that the king was giving up his own life for an insignificant bird. Nevertheless, the king considered his duty to protect the bird to be above everything else. He sat in the scale on the side opposite the pigeon, closed his eyes, and began meditating.

As soon as the king began meditating, the pigeon and the hawk assumed their original divine forms. Both demigods bowed to the king and said, "Oh great king! You are blessed. You deserve all the praise given by Lord Indra. We are convinced that you are a brave and merciful king."

With these words, they praised and saluted the king again and left. The whole court resounded with cheers of joy, "Long live King Megharath". Later on, the soul of King Megharath became the sixteenth Tirthankar, Lord Shäntinäth.

This story teaches us that it is the chief duty of everyone to protect and help those who are less fortunate. A merciful person is someone who is not only influenced by seeing the misery and suffering of others, but goes a step further and attempts to alleviate the pain. He gives financial aid to those who are poor and gives food to those who are hungry and needy. A merciful person would not harm others to save his/her own life, but on the contrary, would sacrifice his/her own life to save the lives of the others.

15 Sage Nandisen

Sage Nandisen was a great ascetic and well versed in the scriptures. He took a vow to serve other monks with utmost devotion. His devotion of serving the monks was popular even in the heavenly abode.

One day, Indra commended his services during an assembly of demigods. One of the demigods was surprised at such high praise for a mere mortal and decided to see the worthiness of sage Nandisen.

The demigods, due to their miraculous power, can assume any form they desire and can reach anywhere in a split second. The demigod arrived at the outskirts of the village and assumed the form of two monks. One became a very old and injured monk while the other became a young and healthy monk.

It was the day sage Nandisen was going to break his fast. He had just returned from collecting Gochari (alms) and was about to break his fast when the young monk came to him and said, "Oh blessed one! There is a very old monk suffering from diarrhea, extreme thirst, and hunger. He is weak and needs your help."

Sage Nandisen helping and serving the old monk

Hearing these words, sage Nandisen immediately got up, took clean water, and went to the old monk. Seeing Nandisen, the old monk raged, "Oh you wretch, I am lying here suffering and you did not even care to see if anyone needs help."

Sage Nandisen was not offended by these words. He had developed virtues of tolerance, forgiveness, and compassion. He calmly replied, "Oh, the best of monks, kindly excuse my oversight. I have brought clean water for you to drink."

He helped the old monk drink the water. He cleaned his clothes, his body, and helped him sit up. The old monk again became irritated. He frowned, "Oh you fool, do you not see that I am too weak to sit? What are you doing to me?"

Sage Nandisen said, "I will help you." After helping the old monk to sit up, he said, "Oh revered monk, if you desire, I shall carry you to the Upäshray (place where monks stay temporarily) where you will be more comfortable."

The monk replied, "Why are you asking me? You may do so if you wish."

Sage Nandisen seated the monk on his shoulders and slowly proceeded towards the Upäshray. He walked slowly, watching every step carefully. The old monk was determined to test him so he increased his own weight gradually. With the increased weight on his shoulder, sage Nandisen began to tremble and he

Heavenly beings praising the compassionate act of Sage Nandisen

almost fell. The old monk said, "Oh you wretch, what is wrong with you? Don't you know how to walk? You are shaking my entire body. Is this the way to serve the sick?"

His words were very rude and harsh, but sage Nandisen was not disturbed at all. He said, "Pardon me. I shall be more careful."

Ignoring the monk's comments he continued walking, and took care not to offend the monk with any more of his actions. On the way, he thought of ways to cure the monk.

He arrived at the Upäshray with the monk. During all this, the old monk was watching sage Nandisen and did not see any change in the helping nature of the sage even after all the aggravation. The old monk turned back into an angel and bowed down at once to sage Nandisen, saying, "You are blessed. Oh sage, you are the illustration of a real monk. You deserve all the praise given by Indra. I am very pleased with you and will grant you whatever you wish."

"Oh heavenly angel, this human life is very precious. Nothing is more valuable than human existence. I am content. I crave for nothing," said sage Nandisen. The heavenly angel bowed his head at the feet of the sage and returned to his abode, applauding the merits of the sage.

This story teaches us the importance of tolerance, discipline, and contentment which are all fundamental values of Jainism. First and foremost, sage Nandisen chose to devote his life to serving monks which is very admirable and requires the utmost level of dedication and discipline. The important point to realize is that sage Nandisen demonstrated his tolerance (abstinence from getting angry) and willingness to serve others before serving himself without even knowing that the demigod was testing him. This means that he was truly dedicated to monks and believed in what he was doing. He also indicated his contentment with the human life when asked for a wish. This contentment is symbolic of the principle of non-possessiveness.

16 King Shripäl and Mayanä-sundari

King Singhrath ruled over Champä-nagar. By his queen, Kamal-prabhä, he had a son named Shripäl. The king died when Shripäl was five years old. King Singhrath's brother Ajitsen was very ambitious and took this opportunity to seize the throne. He was keen on getting rid of Shripäl in order to make his position as king secure. When Kamal-prabhä became aware of Ajitsen's vicious plan, she fled from Champä-nagar along with her son. Learning about her escape, Ajitsen sent his trusted soldiers to pursue her. How long could the poor lady go, especially since she had to run on foot with a young child? As the soldiers got close, she did not know how to save her son. She saw a group of lepers. In desperation, she asked them to take her son into their custody. They warned her about the risk of her son contracting the disease of leprosy from them. However, she had no choice if she wanted to save her son, so she entrusted her son to them.

Shripäl was very bold and handsome. The leper colony became very fond of him and took great care of Shripäl. Ultimately, Shripäl contracted leprosy. When he became a youth, the people made him their leader, and named him Umar Ränä. Under his leadership, the group traveled from place to place and one day arrived at Ujjayini city, the capital of Mälwä region.

King Prajäpäl was ruling there. He and queen Rupsundari had two daughters named Sursundari and Mayanä-sundari. They were very beautiful and intelligent. The king loved both of them and made adequate arrangements for their training in the arts and crafts. The girls mastered all of them in due course. Once the king decided to test their knowledge and called them in the assembly hall. He asked a number of questions to Sursundari who gave satisfactory replies to all of them. At the end, the king asked her by whose favor she got all her skills and also the amenities and luxuries that she enjoyed. The girl humbly replied that she gained all that by the king's favor. The king was pleased with her replies and decided to reward her appropriately.

Then he asked several questions to Mayanä-sundari. She too gave satisfactory replies to all his questions. At the end, the king asked her the same question that he had asked Sursundari. He had expected Mayanä to give an identical reply and thus please him. But Mayanä had total faith in the religious philosophy she had studied at length. She therefore replied:

"O father! The great king! With due respect to you, all the comfort that you provide me are only because of my meritorious (Punya) Karma. Every one gets whatever is written in his or her destiny due to his or her Karma. You yourself cannot give or take away anything."

Everything that she had received had been the result of her Karma. She must have earned good Karma in the past that resulted in the happy situations that she was undergoing. If she did not have that Karma to her credit, no one could bestow happiness on her. The king was exasperated to hear the unexpected reply. He repeatedly asked her to consider how she could have obtained anything but for his generosity. Mayanä replied that everything right from her being born as his daughter up to her present situation could occur solely as a consequence of her good or bad Karmas, and no one or nothing could have made any difference.

The king grew angry from her unexpected persistence. He could not believe that the girl could have received anything but for his favor. He could not believe that everything happens according to one's own

Karma. He therefore decided to teach her a lesson - the hard way. He asked his men to find the ugliest man in Ujjayini. The men spotted Umar Ränä and brought him to the court. In utter disdain, the king instantly got Mayanä married to Umar. He gave them some basic things and a small house and asked Mayanä to undergo the result of her Karma. Rupsundari, the mother queen, was very unhappy at the sudden turn of events in her daughter's life, but she could not speak against her husband's will. On the other hand, the king looked for a suitable match for Sursundari in appreciation of her replies and got her married to prince Aridaman of Shankhapuri.

Princess Mayanä marrying Shripäl

Mayanä was deeply religious. She accepted Shripäl in the guise of Umar as her husband and took care of him. She went to temples and heard the sermons of monks (Sädhus) along with him. One day Mayanä-sundari and her husband went to see Jain Ächärya Munichandra and talked about their problems and his leprosy disease. The Ächärya was a well-known scholar of the time. He advised them to go through the penance of Äyambil Oli, known as Navapad (nine pious entities) penance, which can cure all types of diseases. They had to do this for four and half years which results in Nine Äyambil – Oli (one every six months).

The Navapad Ärädhanä (pujä) is observed by meditation and practicing a penance called Äyambil. One meditates upon Arihanta, Siddha, Ächärya, Upädhyäy, Sädhus (Pancha Paramesthi), Jnän (knowledge), Darshan (faith), Chäritra (conduct), and Tapa (penance) known as Navapad. Äyambil is observed by having only one meal a day of very plain food without any spices, milk, sugar, salt, oil, butter, fruits or vegetables. This penance and meditation are to be observed for nine days, twice a year, during the month of March/April (Chaitra) and September/October (Ashwin).

Accordingly, Mayanä and Shripäl devoutly observed Navapad worship and penance with all its vitality. The result was miraculous: Shripäl's skin disease started fading. In due course, he got totally cured of leprosy and regained the skin that he had before contracting the disease. Now he looked like the handsome prince that he had been. Mayanä was very happy and blessed her Karma for that change too. Since the change was apparently brought about by devotion to Navapad and practicing the penance, both of them continued to observe it even after that.

Once, while they were at a temple, queen Rupsundari saw them. She was shocked to see that her daughter

Shripäl and Mayanä are ardent worshippers of Navapad

was with a handsome man instead of the leper with whom she was married. Mayanä understood her anxiety and explained in detail everything that had happened. Rupsundari was extremely pleased to hear that. She told the king that Mayanä's persistence about the theory of Karma had proved right. The king could also see the truth. Deep in his heart he used to curse himself for bringing misery in his lovely daughter's life. Now he too became happy and invited his daughter and son-in-law to stay with him in the palace. Shripäl's real identity was revealed to all, and luckily his mother arrived at the palace and stayed with them.

Once there was a royal procession in which Shripäl was seated on an elephant along with the king. During the procession someone pointed a finger at Shripäl and asked a relative who he was. The man replied that he was the son-in-law of the king. Shripäl heard that. He became sad that he was being identified by his relationship with his father-in-law. He felt that one should gain fame from one's own efforts and not from association with relatives. He, therefore, secured permission from Mayanä and the king and set off by himself on an auspicious day.

He traveled far and wide, visited many places, and boldly faced the adversities that he encountered. During that period, he did not forsake his devotion to Navapad. Consequently, he successfully survived all the ordeals. As was the custom at that time, he married many girls and acquired a lot of wealth and many followers. Equipped with that, he came back and camped outside Ujjayini. His army was so large that it virtually surrounded the city. King Prajäpäl thought that some enemy had come with a large force to conquer Ujjayini. He came to the camp and was pleased to recognize his son-in-law. Shripäl entered the city where he was given a hero's welcome. His mother and Mayanä were anxiously awaiting his arrival and were very happy to see him.

Shripäl happily spent some time with Mayanä who was dearest to him. Then he decided to get back his original kingdom of Champä-nagar. He sent a message to his uncle Ajitsen to leave the throne that he had seized. Ajitsen was however too proud to give it up. Therefore, Shripäl invaded Champä-nagar with his vast army. Ajitsen put up a tough fight. However, his army was not a match for Shripäl's. In the tough fight Ajitsen was captured and Champä-nagar was taken over by Shripäl. He then gracefully released his uncle from captivity. Ajitsen now felt that his days were almost over, and he decided to renounce the worldly life. Thereafter Shripäl happily passed the rest of his life as king of Champä-nagar.

This story describes the faith of Mayanä Sundari on the philosophy of Karma and her devotion to Navapad. It stresses the importance of her effort and determination to change her fate.

Mayanä understood the nature of Karma. However, she was not content with her fate. She and her husband, Shripäl, exerted their own efforts into prayer and practice to improve his condition and were ultimately successful. They accepted that Karma had put them into their current condition, but they also knew that they could change their future if they only put effort into acquiring good Karmas and destroying bad Karmas.

Happiness or misery is a state of mind regardless of the situation one is in. If you think you are miserable, then you will be miserable. Full faith in the theory of Karma is essential to be content and happy.

17 Ilächikumär

In ancient times, there lived a wealthy businessman named Dhandatta in the town of Ilävardhan. His wife Ilächi gave birth to a very lovable and handsome boy. Being the only son, the parents deliberately kept him nameless as was the custom in those days. As the son of Ilächi he came to be known as Ilächiputra. He was raised with loving care and attention and never lacked any luxuries. He grew up to be a handsome youth and was eventually known as Ilächikumär. His parents felt it was time to find a wife for him. They did not need to look very far. Since they were a prosperous family and Ilächikumär was their only son, many families wanted their daughters to marry him. His parents prepared a list of selected names and asked Ilächikumär to choose the one that he liked the most. However, Ilächikumär could not make a selection.

One day a party of acrobats came to Ilävardhan. In those days, there were no stadiums where acrobats could perform. They performed their skills for their audience on the open streets. Beating drums to announce their arrival, the acrobats planted poles in an open square off the main street and connected them with ropes. Many people assembled there to watch the show. The acrobats climbed the pole one after another and started demonstrating their skills by performing on the rope. They were walking and jumping over the high rope, fascinating the people with their performance. Attracted by the commotion, Ilächikumär also went to watch the show. While watching the performance of the acrobats, his attention was drawn to the young daughter of the chief acrobat. She was very beautiful and was dancing very gracefully to the tune of the drums with bells on her feet. Ilächikumär was so mesmerized by her beauty and charm that he could not take his eyes off her.

At the end of the show, the acrobats descended the rope and started collecting money from the people who had assembled for the show. People were very pleased with the performance and paid handsomely. After collecting a large amount of money, the acrobats left the square to camp for the night and everyone else went home. Ilächikumär also returned home. But his mind was still on the beautiful girl he had seen that day. At dinner, his parents found him silent and unresponsive to their efforts to converse with him. His parents had never seen him so dazed. His father questioned his absent-mindedness but he did not answer. After dinner when his mother persisted on the reason for his silence, he finally replied that his heart was attracted to the acrobat girl and he wanted to marry her.

His mother was taken aback to hear that. She said that she could find him a very beautiful and lovable girl from a high caste and respectable family and asked him to forget the lower caste acrobat girl. Ilächikumär replied that he had never met any other girl who attracted him and he wanted to marry that girl. Acknowledging his resolve on the matter, she told her husband about their son's intentions. Dhandatta was shocked to hear this. He tried to dissuade his son from his intention but Ilächikumär remained firm. Dhandatta was a sensible man. He could see that Ilächikumär would not be at peace without that girl. He did not want to lose his son for the sake of prestige. He therefore called the chief of acrobats and requested him to give his daughter in marriage to Ilächikumär.

The acrobat refused because he was bound by the convention of his tribe. Dhandatta thought that he might be looking for money for the girl. He therefore offered to give as much wealth as the acrobat wanted for agreeing to marry his daughter to his son. The acrobat, however, declined the offer and replied that he could not break the convention. Dhandatta then asked him about his tribal convention. The acrobat said that he could give his daughter only to the person who could win an award from a royal court by pleasing the king with his acrobatic skill and would then give dinner to his community from the prize money. Dhandatta was disappointed to hear that because it was apparently impossible for his son to fulfill that condition. He explained to his wife what had happened. She called her son and said that the girl would only marry an expert acrobat and asked him to forget her.

Ilächikumär was silent but his mind was racing with thoughts. He felt that he would not be able to live happily without the girl and was willing to make any sacrifice for her. He was even prepared to learn acrobatic skills for that purpose. His parents misunderstood his silence as disappointment and felt that in time he would recover. They tried to divert his attention to other matters to help him forget and Ilächikumär allowed them to believe that they were succeeding. But his mind was made up. When the acrobat group decided to leave the town of Ilävardhan, Ilächikumär secretly left his home and joined the acrobat group.

He discarded his fancy clothes and put on an acrobat's uniform. He started learning their skill. He was smart and diligently learned the acrobatic skills. The girl fell in love with him and helped him to learn the skills. With her help he easily mastered the skill and soon became an expert acrobat. When the group reached the city of Benätat, he requested the father of the girl to organize a show at the royal court. Thereafter, the chief went to the young king and requested him to watch the performance of the young acrobat and to award him a suitable prize for his skills.

The king agreed and the acrobats erected the poles in the compound of the royal palace where the officers of the state and the elite of the city were invited to watch the performance. The king occupied his seat in the balcony of the palace. Bowing to him, Ilächikumär went over the pole. Jumping onto the rope he started displaying his acrobatic skills. He walked on the rope with ease and grace. He also performed risky jumps and somersaults. It was a superb performance. No one had ever seen such acrobatic feats. Everyone was highly impressed with his skill. Ilächikumär felt gratified by the appreciation of the people. He thought that it was enough to please the king as well. He came down, and bowed to the king again and requested an appropriate award.

During the performance, however, the king's attention had been diverted by the beautiful girl. She fascinated him. He saw how she gazed lovingly at Ilächikumär throughout the performance. He thought that he could easily gain her if he somehow got rid of Ilächikumär. The chief acrobat approached the king and asked if he had enjoyed the performance. The king pretended that his mind had been occupied with problems of the state and he was not able to give his full attention to the performance. He requested Ilächikumär to show his skill again. Accordingly, Ilächikumär got on the rope again and displayed his skills. At the end of the show, the king pretended to be drowsy and asked him to repeat the performance. Ilächikumär could not believe it. He suspected that there was something wrong. However, since he was still eager to accomplish his cherished goal of marrying the girl, he decided to try again.

He started the ropewalk once again. He triumphantly looked around. While up there, he noticed a beautiful woman offering sweet food to a young monk. She was in the prime of her youth and was very attractive and highly graceful. What surprised Ilächikumär was that the monk was completely unaffected by her beauty. He compared it to his own situation. He had changed his entire life for the beauty of one girl and the monk was impervious to the lovely woman in front of him. He was amazed by the self-control and detached attitude of the monk towards the beautiful woman. What power kept the monk aloof in the presence of that woman? In addition, while remaining aloof, peace radiated from his face! This detachment of the monk raised a succession of thoughts in the mind of Ilächikumär.

"Why do I not feel detachment in the presence of a beautiful young girl?" He also wondered why the young king had asked him to repeat his performances. He suspected that the king must be attracted to the girl and must be waiting for him to fall from the rope. "If I fall from the rope, I would be badly hurt and would not be able to perform acrobatic feats. In that case I will never be able to marry the girl for whom I have abandoned my home and my parents." He realized that the happiness he was looking for was an illusion. He began to recall his early religious training when he had been exposed to religious principles. He had learned about the soul within the body and its immense capabilities. He realized that his achievements as an acrobat must have been due to that inner capability. The monk could remain unaffected because he remained tuned to his soul and stayed vigilant about the pitfalls. "As an acrobat I have to remain constantly vigilant because the slightest unawareness on my part can result in a fall from the high rope and possibly in my death. Why then should I not use the same vigilance for the sake of spiritual upliftment?"

Ilächikumar realizing the futility of attachment while observing a monk's action

He had treaded a long path of spiritual pursuit in an earlier life. The impact of that achievement was lying subdued within him, waiting for an opportunity to manifest itself. The sight of the monk provided the needed catalyst. He became fully awakened to the realization that he was a soul and that all the other situations were simply an illusion. While on the rope, he dwelt deep into his Self and attained omniscience or Keval-jnän. Then he quietly climbed down the pole and bid farewell to every one as he left the place.

The focus of this story is on the principle of detachment. Attachment to materialistic things, people or feelings often causes misery to others and to us. We should strive to minimize our attachment to the outer world (i.e. detach ourselves) and focus on our inner self. Attachment is an obstacle in the path of self-realization. The monk's detachment towards the beautiful woman guided Ilächikumär onto the right path.

18 Monk Kurgadu

In ancient times, there lived a businessman named Dhandatta, who was highly religious. He also raised his son to be very religious. Once Dharmaghosh-suri, the highly enlightened Ächärya of that time, came to the town where Dhandatta lived. Dhandatta took his son to listen to his sermon. The boy was so impressed by the Ächärya's sermon that he decided to become his disciple. Accordingly, he renounced worldly life and became a monk at a very young age. The Ächärya realized that the boy had tremendous potential to be a great Jain monk. He therefore renamed him Kulaguru. In the native language of that area he came to be known as Kurgadu.

Kurgadu studied the holy books and correctly comprehended their essence. He realized the role of Karma in the life of every being and thereby learned to maintain a high level of equanimity. He rigorously observed the code of conduct for monks. However, he could not overcome one problem. It was difficult for him to stay hungry and so he could not fast. He needed to eat at least once a day. Even during Paryushan Parva he could not fast even for a single day. As he ate his food on the days of Parva, he felt miserable and regretted that he was not able to fast. He attributed his inability to fast to his previous Karmas. When the other monks observed their fasts, he praised them and rendered every type of service to them. He wished in his heart that he could someday observe fasts.

It was during one monsoon season that an event occurred that changed his situation. During the monsoon season, Jain monks forgo traveling and remain in one place for the duration of the monsoons. Paryushan Parva falls during the monsoon season. During this Paryushan Parva, Ächärya Dharmaghosh-suri, along with many of his disciples including Muni Kurgadu, was in town. Many of the monks undertook long fasts, some extending more than a month. Kurgadu felt disappointed that he could not observe such austerities. Especially on the day of Samvatsari he wished that he could observe a day long fast. He began the day in an earnest effort to avoid eating for one day. However, before noon he felt very hungry and could not do without food. He was surprised at the kind of Karma he had acquired that he could not fast even for a day! He reluctantly approached the Guru and begged his permission to go for alms. The Guru lovingly tried to persuade him to go without food for at least one day. He should be inspired to observe a fast at least for that day, especially when all other monks were on long fasts. Kurgadu humbly replied that he did wish to observe a fast and very much regretted his inability to fast. The Guru pitied his miserable fate and compassionately allowed him to go for alms.

Kurgadu went for alms and accepted the food that was offered to him. Returning, he presented the alms to his Guru as part of the monks' code of conduct and begged his permission to eat. He did all this in modesty. Guru gave his permission but other monks made negative remarks. Kurgadu was eating on an auspicious day and felt sorry that he was acquiring unwholesome Karmas on the day of Samvatsari. They unsympathetically said that he did not deserve to be a monk. Kurgadu listened to the remarks quietly. He went to a corner and most reluctantly started to eat.

While eating, Kurgadu dwelt deeply on the inability of his body to remain without food even for a day. Well read as he was, he could see that it must be the result of his previous Karma. He understood that all Karmas are shed after extending the appropriate consequence and this Karma too would be shed. He made up his mind to passively accept what had been ordained by his Karma. Because of his study of the scriptures, he had gained insight about the true nature of his soul. Despising himself for not observing a fast was functioning as a handicap to the full realization of that true nature. Now, his willingness to accept what was a physical limitation endowed him the insight of distinguishing the nature of soul from the varying states of the body and mind. That gave rise to the manifestation of the true nature of the soul. His realization was strong enough to destroy all the defiling Karmas on the spot and he gained omniscience (Keval-jnän) immediately while he was eating.

Muni Kurgadu achieves Enlightenment

When one attains omniscience, heavenly beings arrive to offer their obeisance. When other monks saw the heavenly beings coming towards them, they felt that the heavenly beings were coming to praise them for their severe austerities. Instead, they turned to Kurgadu and offered their obeisance to him. No one could understand why those observing severe austerity were left out while the one who could not observe it at all had gained full enlightenment.

In amazement, they went to Dharmaghosh-suri and asked him the reason for what had happened. The Ächärya said that all of them were feeling very proud of their austerities and were unnecessarily disapproving of Kurgadu for not observing a fast. Thereby they were smeared by perception obscuring Karma that obscured right perception. He urged them to bear in mind that the primary purpose of observing austerities or any other religious practice was to gain modesty that leads to right perception and in turn helps to attain equanimity. They had misjudged Kurgadu who had realized the essence of religion. Earlier he had acquired obstructing Karma that did not allow him to observe the austerity. He felt sad and sincerely repented for that Karma which had become operative in his current life. By properly comprehending the role of Karma he acquired right perception. He regretted those Karmas but he was bearing the consequence of it with equanimity. This helped in wiping out the previously acquired Karmas without incurring new bondage.

All the monks realized that they were indulging in unnecessary vanity that obstructed right perception. The Ächärya also explained that the soul had nothing to do with the state and activities of the body. The body is obtained as a consequence of the operative Karma and should be used simply as an instrument for realizing the true nature of soul. It can be an effective instrument only if it is used purposefully. Understanding the true nature of the soul is the essence of religion and it is the only thing worth pursuing in this life. We should never look down upon anyone who cannot observe austerities and penance or one who cannot follow the religious principles as much as others. Rather than putting these people down, one must encourage them to do so with compassion and realize that it is due to the Karmas of that person that they are unable to do so. One must never be proud of the austerities that one is able to perform.

Part IV
Stories during Bhagawän Mahävir's Life

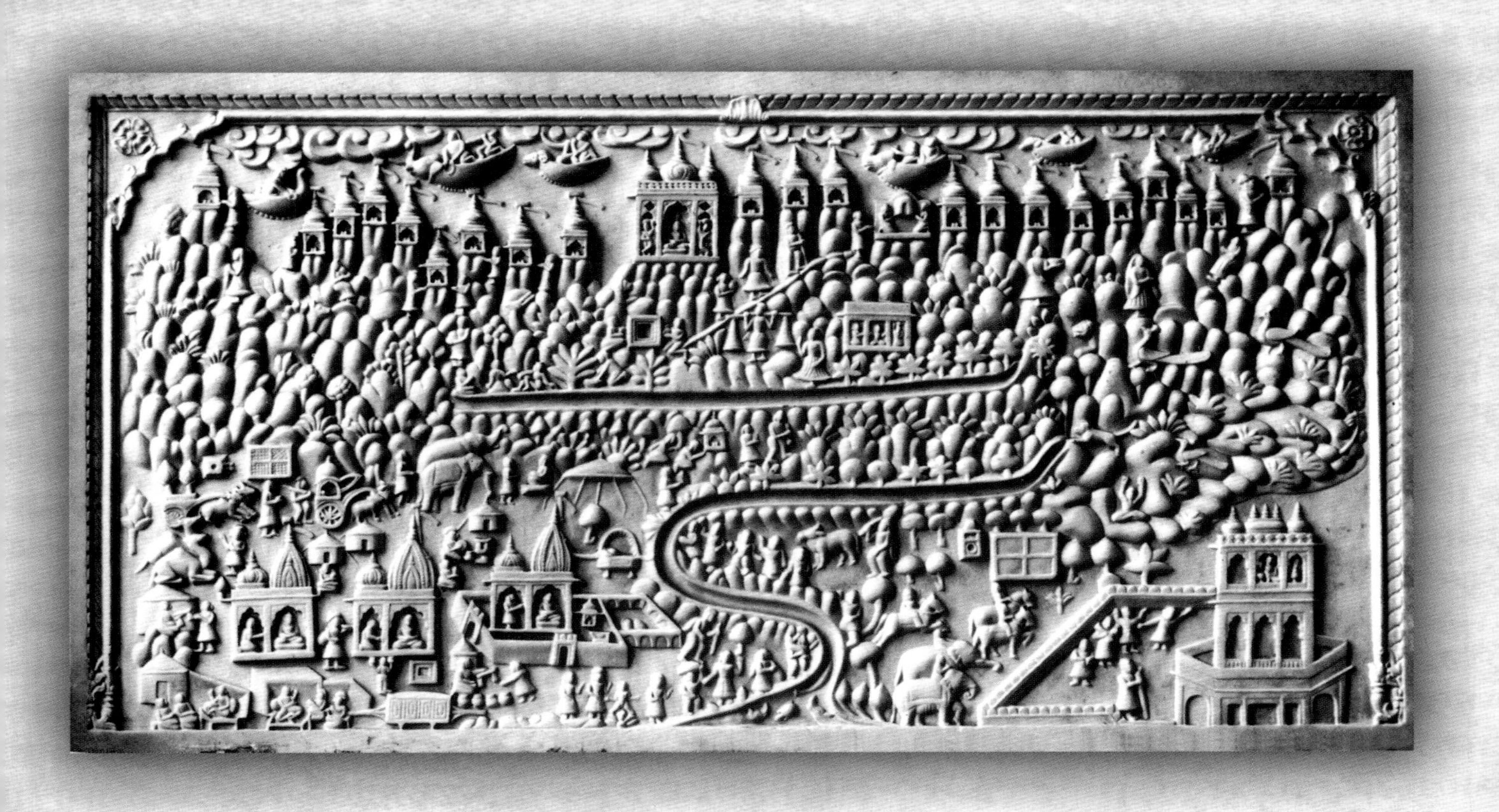

"That Which subdues passions, leads to bliss and fosters friendliness is called knowledge"

- Mulächär (5/71)

19 Mahävir-swämi and the Cow Herder

One day as Mahävir-swämi was going from one place to another, he stopped near a big tree to meditate. While he was meditating, a cow herder came with his cows. He needed someone to look after his cows so he could go for some errands. He asked Mahävir-swämi if he would look after his cows for a few hours. Mahävir-swämi was in deep meditation and did not respond to the cow herder. However, the cow herder went away thinking that Mahävir-swämi had heard him and would look after his cows.

In the meantime, the cows started wandering away looking for grass. A few hours later, the cow herder returned and found all his cows were missing. He asked Mahävir-swämi, "Where are my cows? What did you do with them?" Mahävir-swämi was still in meditation and did not reply. The herder started wondering where the cows could have gone. Since Mahävir-swämi did not reply, the cow herder searched for them everywhere but could not find them. While he was looking for the cows, the cows returned to the place where Mahävir-swämi was meditating.

When the cow herder came back, to his amazement all his cows were standing near Mahävir-swämi. Mahävir-swämi was still meditating. The cow herder became very angry with Mahävir-swämi because he thought that Mahävir-swämi had been hiding his cows. Therefore, he took out his rope and was about to whip Mahävir-swämi with it. Just then, an angel from heaven came down and held the rope.

Indra preventing an ignorant cowherd from assaulting Bhagawän Mahävir

"Can you not see that Mahävir-swämi is in deep meditation?" the angel asked.

"But he tricked me!" said the cow herder. The angel replied, "He is in meditation and did not hear you. He was prince Vardhamän before becoming a monk. He did not do anything to your cows. You would have acquired bad Karmas for hurting him."

The cow herder realized that he had made a mistake. He apologized to Mahävir-swämi and went away silently.

Then, the angel bowed down to Mahävir-swämi and requested, "Oh Lord, I would like to be at your service as you will have to undergo many hardships during your spiritual journey."

Bhagawän denying Indra's protection

Mahävir-swämi answered, "One cannot progress spiritually and attain Keval-jnän using others help and support. To attain Keval-jnän and become an Arihanta one has to undertake all the efforts personally on the journey towards omniscience and liberation."

The angel went back to heaven feeling happy that he could stop Mahävir-swämi's suffering. Mahävir did not have any bad feelings towards the cow herder because he held no anger towards anyone.

We should not make hasty decisions because we could be wrong. One should think from all perspectives before acting. Secondly, we should not hurt anyone for any reason, but should forgive instead of displaying anger. This is the way we can stop the inflow of bad Karmas to our souls.

20 Chandkaushik

This is a story about Bhagawän Mahävir when he was a monk. He used to fast, meditate, and perform penance. He was traveled bare feet from place to place and village to village. Bhagawän Mahävir once decided to go to the village of Vachala. On his way, he would have to go through a forest where a poisonous snake named Chandkaushik lived. It was said that Chandkaushik could kill a person or animal just by casting an evil and angry glance at them. All the people of the villages near that forest lived in absolute fear.

When the villagers learned about Mahävir's intention to pass through the forest, they begged him to take another longer route. However, Mahävir had no fear. He practiced supreme non-violence. He had no hatred towards anyone and considered fear and hatred as violence to oneself. He was at peace with himself and all other living beings. There was a glow of serenity and compassion on his face. He convinced the

Bhagawän Mahävir enlightening a poisonous snake - Chandkaushik

people that everything would be all right and he proceeded to the forest where Chandkaushik lived. After a while, he noticed the beautiful green grass fading. The forest looked like a desert. Trees and plants were dead so he thought that this must be near the area where Chandkaushik lived. Mahävir stopped there to meditate. Peace, tranquility, and compassion for the well-being of each and every living being flowed from Mahävir's heart.

Chandkaushik sensed that someone had come near his land and so he came out of his burrow. To his surprise, he saw a man standing there. He became furious, thinking, "How dare he come this close to my land?" Chandkaushik started hissing to threaten Lord Mahävir. He did not understand Lord Mahävir's tranquility. He became angry, came closer to the Lord and swayed his head, ready to strike. He saw no sign that this man would be threatened or would run away. This made Chandkaushik even angrier and he blew poisonous venom towards Lord Mahävir three times. The venom neither affected Lord Mahävir nor disturbed his meditation. So Chandkaushik became even more irritated and bit Lord Mahävir's toe. When he looked at the man again, he was surprised to see that not only had nothing happened to him, but instead of blood, milk flowed from his toe.

Bhagawän Mahävir opened his eyes. He was calm and there was no fear or anger on his face. He looked at Chandkaushik and said, "Calm down, Calm down, Chandkaushik. Realize what you are doing." There was love and affection in those words. Chandkaushik calmed down and felt as if he had seen this kind of monk before. He suddenly remembered his two previous lives. Chandkaushik then realized the truth of life and what anger and ego from his last two lives had done to him. He bowed his head respectfully to the Lord.

Chandkaushik peacefully retreated to his hole with his head inside while portion of his body remained outside the hole. After a while when the people came to know that Chandkaushik was no longer harmful to anyone, they came to see him out of curiosity. They saw him lying quietly. Some started worshipping him by offering milk and food, while some were still furious because he had killed their loved ones. They threw stones and beat him with wooden sticks. Blood, milk, and food attracted ants. Chandkaushik willingly suffered the biting and beating and remained at peace with no trace of anger. He died after a few days. The self-restraint and control of his feelings destroyed many of his bad Karmas. Therefore, at the end of his life he was born in heaven.

Fear, hatred, and ego are violence to one's self and not to anyone else. Chandkaushik depicts this from the anger and ego he had committed during his past lives. Self-realization through the help of Bhagawän Mahävir made him realize his mistake and led him to repent for his deeds. This ultimately washed away his bad Karmas and led him to heaven. Learning from this story, we should remain calm and avoid anger, ego, and all forms of violence. We should be fearless of evil and approach them with tranquility.

21 Chandanbälä

Once upon a time, there was a beautiful princess named Vasumati. She was the daughter of King Dadhivähan and Queen Dhärini of the city of Champäpuri in the state of Bihar, India.

One day, a war broke out between King Dadhivähan and King Shatänik of the nearby city of Kaushämbi. King Dadhivähan was defeated in the war and he had to run away in despair. When princess Vasumati and Queen Dhärini learned that they had lost the war, they decided to escape. While they were running away from the palace, a soldier from the enemy's army spotted and captured them. Princess Vasumati and her mother were scared. They did not know what the soldier would do to them. He told the queen that he would marry her and sell Vasumati. Upon hearing this, the queen went into shock and died. He then took Vasumati to Kaushämbi to sell her.

When it was Vasumati's turn to be sold in the slave market, a merchant named Dhanävah happened to be passing by. He saw Vasumati being sold and looking at her noble face, he realized that she was not an ordinary slave girl. He thought she might have been separated from her parents and if she were sold as a slave, what would her fate be? Therefore, out of compassion Dhanävah bought Vasumati and took her home. On the way, he asked her, "Who are you and what has happened to your parents?" Vasumati did not reply. Dhanävah then told her not to be afraid and that he would treat her as his daughter.

When they reached home, the merchant told his wife, Moolä, about Vasumati. "My dear," he said, "I have brought this girl home. She has not said anything about her past. Please treat her like our daughter." Vasumati was relieved. She thanked the merchant and his wife with respect. The merchant's family was very happy with her. They named her Chandanbälä since she would not tell anyone her real name.

While staying at the merchant's house, Chandanbälä's attitude was like that of a daughter. This made the merchant very happy. Moolä, on the other hand, started wondering what her husband would do with Chandanbälä. She thought that he may marry her because of her beauty. Therefore, Moolä was getting uncomfortable with the idea of having Chandanbälä around.

One day, when the merchant came home from work, the servant who usually washed his feet was not there. Chandanbälä noticed this and was delighted to have a chance to wash his feet for all the fatherly love he had given her. While she was busy washing the merchant's feet, her hair slipped out of the hairpin. The merchant saw this and felt that her beautiful long hair might get dirty, so he lifted her hair and clipped it back. Moolä saw this and was outraged. She felt that her doubts about Chandanbälä were true. Moolä decided to get rid of Chandanbälä as soon as possible.

Mula being suspicious of Chandanbälä's innocent act

When Dhanävah went on a three-day business trip, his wife used this opportunity to get rid of Chandanbälä. She called a barber right away to shave off Chandanbälä's beautiful hair. Then she tied Chandanbälä's legs with heavy shackles and locked her in a room away from the main area of the house. She told the other servants not to tell Dhanävah where Chandanbälä was or she would do the same to them. Then Moolä left and went to her parent's house.

When Dhanävah returned from his trip he did not see Moolä or Chandanbälä. He asked the servants about them. The servants told him that Moolä was at her parent's house, but they did not tell him where Chandanbälä was because they were scared of Moolä. He asked the servants in a worried tone, "Where is my daughter Chandanbälä? Please speak up and tell the truth." Still nobody said a word. He was very upset and did not know what to do. After a few minutes an older servant thought, "I am an old woman and will soon die anyway. What is the worst thing Moolä can do to me?" So out of compassion for Chandanbälä and sympathy for the merchant she told him everything that Moolä had done to Chandanbälä.

She took the merchant to the room where Chandanbälä was locked up. Dhanävah unlocked the door and saw Chandanbälä. He was shocked when he saw her. He told Chandanbälä, "My dear daughter, I will get you out of here. You must be hungry. Let me find some food for you." He went to the kitchen to find food for her. He found that there was no food left except for some boiled lentils in a pan. The merchant took the pan of lentils to Chandanbälä. He told her that he was going to get a blacksmith to cut the heavy shackles and left.

Chandanbälä was thinking about how her life had changed. She started wondering how fate can change a person's life from riches to almost helplessness. Chandanbälä decided that she would like to make an offering of food to a monk or nun before eating. She got up, walked to the door, and stood there with one foot outside and one inside.

To her surprise, she saw Lord Mahävir walking towards her. She said, "Oh revered Lord, please accept this food." However, Lord Mahävir had taken a vow to fast until a person who met certain conditions offered him food. Some of his conditions were:

- The person offering the food should be a princess
- She should be bald
- She should be in shackles
- She should offer boiled lentils, with one foot inside and the other foot outside the house
- She should have tears in her eyes

Lord Mahävir looked at her and noticed that one of his predefined conditions was still missing. She met all the conditions except the one about having tears in her eyes, and therefore Lord Mahävir walked away. Chandanbälä was very sad that Lord Mahävir did not accept alms from her and started crying. Tears streamed down her face. Crying, she again requested Lord Mahävir to accept the alms. Lord Mahävir saw the tears in her eyes and came back to accept the food knowing that all his conditions were now met. Chandanbälä offered the lentils to Lord Mahävir and was very happy.

As Lord Mahävir had fasted for five months and twenty-five days, heavenly beings celebrated the end of Lord Mahävir's fast. By magical power, Chandanbälä's shackles broke, her hair grew back, and she was again dressed as a princess. There was music and celebration that drew the attention of King Shatänik. He came to see Chandanbälä with his family, ministers, and many other people. Sampul, a servant from her father's kingdom, recognized Chandanbälä. He walked towards her, bowed and broke out in tears. King Shatänik asked, "Why are you crying?" Sampul replied, "My Lord, this is Vasumati, the princess of Champäpuri, daughter of King Dadhivähan and Queen Dhärini." The king and queen now recognized her and invited her to live with them.

Later, when Lord Mahävir attained Keval-jnän (perfect knowledge) he reestablished the fourfold order of the Jain Sangha. At that time, Chandanbälä took Dikshä and became the first nun (Sädhvi). She became the head nun of the Jain order. Later on, she attained Keval-jnän and liberation from the cycle of life and death.

Bhagawän Mahävir accepting alms from Chandanbälä

We can learn about a number of behaviors that are cited in this story. Moolä's heart was blinded by jealously and therefore she did not understand Chandanbälä's plight, or the role of a mother and the compassion of a father. This led her to do terrible things resulting in bad Karma. This depicts the destructive power of jealously and why we should avoid it. Next, the selfless old servant who told Dhanävah about what had occurred. She did this out of compassion and risked her own demise at the hands of Moolä. This good Karma will bind to her soul as Punya and demonstrates the principles of Jainism. Similarly, Dhanävah's compassion and treatment of Chandanbälä supports the proper role of a father and the willingness to help an orphan. Lastly, Chandanbälä's offering of food to Lord Mahävir, despite her own pitiful situation, is very selfless and comes from the heart. Following the principles of Jainism ultimately led Chandanbälä to the path of liberation.

22 Nails in the Ears - Last Calamity

Twelve years of meditation and penance passed with great success for Lord Mahävir. His life was exemplary. He put forth unsurpassable examples of truth, non-violence, forgiveness, compassion, fearlessness, yoga and true knowledge.

In the thirteenth year he faced another calamity. Near the village of Shammani he stood in a meditation posture. Just as at the beginning of his asceticism, he met a cowherd who left his oxen in the care of Lord Mahävir.

The cowherd went into the village and returned a little later. The oxen had drifted away while grazing. Not finding his oxen, he asked, "Ascetic, where are my oxen?"

A cowherd poking wooden pegs in Bhagawän Mahävir's ears

Mahävir was in deep meditation and unaware of all this. The cowherd asked again, and once again he did not get any response. He was irritated and shouted, "You hypocrite! Are you deaf, don't you hear anything?"

Mahävir still did not respond. The cowherd became very angry, "You pretender, it seems that both your ears are useless. Wait a minute; I will fix your ears." He picked long nail like thorns from a nearby shrub and pierced the ears of Mahävir deeply by hammering the thorns in.

Even such excruciating agony did not move Mahävir from his meditation; neither did it evoke any feeling of anger or aversion in him.

Completing his meditation he went to the village for alms. He arrived at the door of a trader named Siddhärtha. A doctor friend of the trader was sitting with him. Both of them gave food to Mahävir-swämi with due respect.

The doctor told Siddhärtha, "Friend, the face of this monk has a divine glow but there is a shade of tiredness too. Some inner pain is visible in his eyes. I feel this great sage suffers from some inner agony."

Siddhärtha replied, "Friend, if such a great sage suffers from some kind of pain, we should immediately go with him and treat him."

Bhagawän Mahävir calmly bearing the pain while the pegs are being removed

After taking alms Mahävir-swämi returned. The doctor and Siddhärtha followed him to the place where Mahävir-swämi rested. During examination the doctor found the thorns stuck in his ears. Seeing this, they arranged for the necessary instruments and medicines. They used some medicated oil and tongs and pulled out the thorns. This caused such unbearable agony to Mahävir that an anguished cry was forced out of him. The doctor dressed the wound with some coagulant. Mahävir continued to stand there calm and quiet in deep meditation.

In each incident of difficulty, we see the conquest of Mahävir's soul and mind over his physical pain and suffering. His meditation and penance purified his soul. It helped him to separate himself from perishable and mortal worldly things, and concentrate on the liberation of his immortal soul.

23 Meghakumär

King Shrenik of Magadha region in the State of Bihar, India had a beautiful queen named Dhärini. Once while she was sleeping, she dreamt of a white elephant entering her mouth. She immediately woke up and told the king about her dream. King Shrenik knew that it was an auspicious dream. He called the dream experts who predicted that the queen would give birth to a very handsome and intelligent son who will excel in everything. The king and queen were very pleased to hear this.

During the third month of her pregnancy, queen Dhärini had an irresistible urge to ride an elephant in the country with the king when the sky is decorated with clouds of colorful hues, lightning is flashing and it is raining. In most parts of India, it rains only during the monsoon season which is usually from June to October. Dhärini, however, had the urge during the off-season. The fulfillment of her urge was therefore a problem. In order to see that her health and well-being were not affected by the unsatisfied urge, the king asked his eldest son Abhaykumär, who was also the Prime Minister of the state, for a solution to satisfy the queen's urge. Abhaykumär had a friend who could do miracles. The friend arranged events exactly according to Dhärini's urge. She was therefore able to ride on an elephant with the king and satisfy her urge.

Queen Dhärini riding an elephant

In due course Queen Dhärini gave birth to a very handsome and adorable baby boy. Rain in the Indian language is called Megha, so in commemoration of her urge during pregnancy, the boy was named Meghakumär. At the age of 8, he was sent to school where he learned all 72 types of arts and crafts and became an accomplished youth. He got married and enjoyed all the pleasures of worldly life.

Once Lord Mahävir came to Räjgrihi, the capital city of Magadha and stayed in the Gunashil monastery. Almost every resident of Räjgrihi went to listen to His sermons. Meghakumär went as well. The sermon made a lasting impression on him. He realized the transitory nature of worldly situations and decided to renounce his worldly life. His parents were sad to hear about his plan. They tried everything possible to prevent him from renouncing worldly life. However, he remained firm. Nevertheless, in order to satisfy his parents' wish, he agreed to become the king for one day and was ceremoniously crowned king with all the royal pomp. Immediately after that, he left everything, renounced worldly life and became a disciple monk of Lord Mahävir.

At night, as a junior monk, he was given a place to sleep near the entrance. During the night, other monks using the restrooms had to walk past his side. Since no lamps are allowed in the Upäshray (the monks' residence), they happened to trample on his bed and sometimes their feet accidentally touched his body in the dark. Poor Meghakumär could not sleep for the whole night. He had grown up in luxuries. Therefore, it was difficult for him to bear the accidental kicking by the monks, and his bed and body smeared by the dirt. He felt that he could not bear that sort of a miserable life and decided to give up the life of a monk.

In the morning, he went to Lord Mahävir to seek permission to return home. Mahävir was aware of the discomforts that Meghakumär had faced the previous night and told him, "Meghakumär, you do not remember, but let me describe to you the discomforts that you faced during your previous life."

"In your previous life you were Meruprabha, the king of elephants. Once there was a terrible forest fire

Meghakumär in the previous life as an elephant saving a rabbit's life

which you escaped narrowly. You decided to make a shelter that all the animals could use in case of another fire. You cleared up a vast stretch of land by removing all the plants, bushes, and trees. You also weeded out the grass that grew there."

"Once again there was a wild fire in the forest. All the animals came running and took refuge on that stretch. You were also there. During that time, you raised your foot to scratch your body because of an itch. At that very moment, a rabbit jumped into that space. As you tried to put your foot down, you saw the rabbit jump into that space, and you decided to hold your foot up in order to save the rabbit. The fire raged for two and a half days during which you continued to hold your foot up out of compassion for the rabbit."

"At the end of the fire as the animals retreated, you tried to lower your foot. It was so stiff by then that you could not keep your balance and fell down. You felt agonizing pain and could not get up. You spent three days and nights suffering from severe pain. Ultimately you died, and in your next birth you were

Upon death, the elephant is born as Prince Meghakumär

born here as the prince of King Shrenik because of your compassion for the rabbit. If you could face that much distress for the sake of a rabbit and attain this priceless human life in return, how can you not face the accidental kicking and the dirt from the feet of your fellow monks? Do you realize that by renouncing this worldly life and by becoming a monk you have taken the first step towards the long journey of liberation? Remember that all this suffering and happiness are only due to our own Karmas. They are only temporary by their very nature. The everlasting happiness is achieved only upon liberation."

Meghakumär was spellbound by the Lord's words and realized his mistake. He requested the Lord to reinitiate him since he had virtually broken his vow of monkhood by strongly desiring worldly life. The Lord did so and Meghamuni, as he was called thereafter, started leading a rigorous austere life. Fasting for days at a time, he stayed in meditation most of the time in order to eradicate his Karmas. When his body became very weak and he could no longer observe the rigors of ascetic life, he decided to observe the fast until death. This vow is called Sanlekhanä. He fasted for a month on mount Vaibhärgiri near Räjgrihi. Upon death, he was born in heaven. Bhagawän Mahävir has stated to Gautam-swämi that at the end of the heavenly life, Meghakumär would be reborn as a human being and would attain liberation.

Here is a great example of compassion. An elephant bears discomfort and pain to save a little animal. As we are more developed and more rational beings, we should learn from these animals to be helpful to each other. In addition, when one takes an oath to lead the life a monk, one should not revert to a worldly life or even entertain thoughts of doing so. An ascetic life is a very tough and rigorous life which makes one realize and understand the true nature of the soul. In order to achieve this understanding, one must put aside the worldly life permanently because it tends to distort things. Suffering occurs because of one's past Karma, so one should bear it with patience and focus on the soul for self-realization.

24 Aimuttä Muni

Once upon a time in the streets of Polaspur, India, a six-year-old child named Aimuttä was playing with his friends. He was the son of King Vijay and Queen Shrimati. While playing he saw a monk. The monk's name was Gautam-swämi, the chief disciple of Lord Mahävir. He was barefoot and bald. He was going from one house to another to get alms (food). Aimuttä ran to him and invited him to his palace to get food saying this would make his mother and him very happy. Gautam-swämi agreed and they went to the palace. Aimuttä's mother, Queen Shrimati, was standing in the balcony overlooking the garden. She saw Gautam-swämi and Aimuttä coming towards the palace. She was very happy and came down to receive Gautam-swämi. She welcomed him with devotion and said, "Matthaena Vandämi (my salutation to you)." She asked Aimuttä to go and get his favorite food to offer Gautam-swämi. Aimuttä brought ladoos (sweets) and started putting them in the container even though Gautam-swämi said he didn't need that many. Aimuttä was very happy to be offering food to the monk.

As Gautam-swämi started to leave, Aimuttä said, "Your bag is heavy; please let me carry it for you."

Gautam-swämi said, "Aimuttä, I cannot give it to you because it can only be carried by those who have taken Dikshä and have become a monk."

Aimuttä asked, "What is Dikshä?"

Gautam-swämi explained to him that when someone takes a vow of Dikshä he renounces the worldly life, his house, his family, and all other social and economic ties. Then he becomes a monk. People take Dikshä to avoid the accumulation of bad Karma and to attain liberation. In normal everyday living, people are involved in various activities, which cause them to accumulate Karmas. On the other hand, monks and nuns avoid all the activities of householders in order to avoid accumulating these Karmas.

Aimuttä became curious and asked, "Gurudev, you do not commit sins! However, don't you need to eat? Don't you need a place to live? All these activities cause sins which acquire bad Karmas."

Gautam-swämi was pleased with the child's interest to learn more. So he explained, "We take food but we do not accept food which is made specially for us. We stay in a place but we do not own it, and we do not stay there for more than a few days at a time. We do not keep money, and we do not take part in any business or any organization. Thus, as a monk, we do not do any activity that causes sins.

Aimuttä said, "In that case, Gurudev, I want to take Dikshä."

Aimuttä and Gautam-swämi walked to the place where Lord Mahävir was giving a sermon. Aimuttä joined the others to listen to his teachings. In that sermon, Aimuttä learned what life is all about and what one can do if he or she wants to eliminate worldly suffering. Aimuttä expressed his desire to become a monk to Lord Mahävir. Lord Mahävir said, "We cannot give you Dikshä without your parents' permission." Aimuttä replied, "That is easy. I will go home, get their permission and come back."

Aimuttä went home. He told his mother, "Mother, I want to take Dikshä. Remember you used to say that our household life is full of violence and causes sins? Gautam-swämi and Lord Mahävir also said the same. I want to be free of sins. Therefore, please give me permission to take Dikshä."

Aimuttä's mother was surprised by his words. She was happy in her mind for his fear of sins and his desire to take Dikshä because she was a religious woman. However, she wanted to be sure that Aimuttä understood what "taking Dikshä" meant. So she said, "My son, to take Dikshä is a very hard and disciplined life. You will not have a mother or a father to take care of you. How will you be able to handle such suffering?"

Aimuttä said, "Mother, this household life also has a lot of suffering. At least we know that as a monk the suffering will help destroy Karmas and will lead to liberation."

His mother was very happy to hear this. However, she wanted to test Aimuttä's determination further. She said, "Son, why are you in such a hurry? Wait for a while. You need to take care of us when we get old, and you will have your own family too."

Aimuttä said, "Mother, I learned from Lord Mahävir that no one is young or old. I also learned that no one knows what is going to happen tomorrow. No one knows who will die first or last. So why wait and miss the opportunity which is available to me today?"

His mother was very happy that her son fully understood what Dikshä meant and what his desire was.

She said, "Congratulations, my son. I am very proud of you. You will be a good monk. Do not forget that your goal is to attain liberation and be sure to observe ahimsa (non-violence) throughout your life. I give you permission to take Dikshä."

Aimuttä said, "Thank you, Mother. I will remember your advice."

Aimuttä's mother blessed him and wished him success in his new life. She also helped him get permission from his father, King Vijay.

A few days later he took Dikshä and became a monk called "Bälmuni (young monk) Aimuttä."

One day Bälmuni Aimuttä saw some children playing with a paper boat in a water puddle. He became excited about playing and forgot that as a monk he could not play with water. He ran towards the children and asked if he could play with them. The children became excited that a monk wanted to play with them. He took the lid off his container and started playing with it as if it were a boat. He said, "Look, my boat is also sailing." Meanwhile, other monks came there and saw him playing with water. They said, "Bälmuni, what are you doing? Did you forget that as a monk you should not play with water? Playing with water causes harm to many living beings that live in the water. As monks, we have taken a vow not to hurt any living being. You have violated your vow and have accumulated some bad Karmas."

Bälmuni Aimuttä realized his mistake. He immediately started repenting, "Oh! What have I done? I promised my mother that I would not do any sinful activity. These monks were kind enough to remind me of my mistake! What would have happened if these monks had not seen me?" He was truly regretful for what he had done. He left with the other monks. Monks have to recite the Iriyävahiyam Sutra after returning to their place from outside. Therefore, Bälmuni also recited this sutra. When he came to the part:

Pänakkamne, Beeyakkamne, Hariyakkamane, Osäuttinga Panag-Daga-Matti ...

If I have hurt any living beings of water, green grass, and clay, I am asking for forgiveness ...

Bälmuni Aimuttä plying in water

His repentance had no bounds. He was extremely sorry for what he had done. He began thinking, “What did I do? I have hurt so many living beings just for fun. How can I be free of these sins? How will I face Lord Mahävir? Oh living beings, I have caused harm to you. Please forgive me for my sins. I will never commit these sins again.” Because of his sincere repentance, all of his bad Karmas were destroyed and he attained omniscience or Keval-jnän (infinite knowledge). Now he became a Kevali monk.

After this, Kevali Aimuttä Muni went to Lord Mahävir’s assembly and started walking towards the place where other Kevali monks sit. Some senior monks noticed this and told him, “Oh, Aimuttä!! Where are you going? That is the place for Kevali monks to sit. Go over there, where the other monks are sitting.”

Lord Mahävir interrupted them and said, "Monks, you should not disrespect a Kevali monk. Aimuttä Muni is no ordinary monk now. While reciting Iriyävahiyam Sutra, he destroyed all of his destructive (Ghäti) Karmas and became a Kevali."

The monks realized their mistakes, bowed down to him and thought, "There is no age barrier to be an omniscient or Kevali."

At the end of his life, Bälmuni Aimuttä attained liberation.

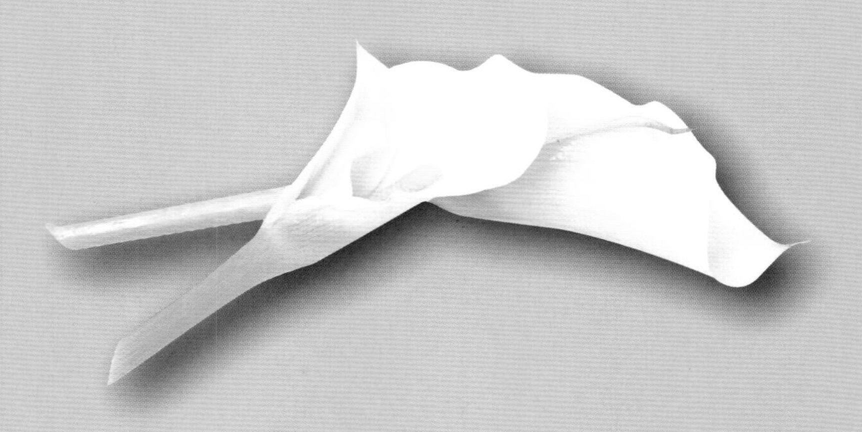

The pursuit and understanding of Jainism has no age limit but is rather driven by one's own true faith, understanding, and the passion to learn and practice the principles of Jainism. All of us make mistakes, which cause bad Karma. Mistakes can be intentional or unintentional. It is possible that Karma resulting from unintentional mistake can be eliminated by true and sincere repentance. However, one should not intentionally make a mistake knowing that they plan to repent for it later. Such repentance will be in vain since it is not true or sincere.

25 Änand Shrävak

Once upon a time, there lived a king named Jitshatru in the city of Vänijya, India. A rich householder named Änand also lived in the same city. He was so rich that he had 4 million gold coins, an equal amount of cash, an equal amount invested in business, lots of jewelry, and many other assets. He also owned 40,000 cows. He was highly respected by the king as well as by the people of Vänijya.

One day Lord Mahävir visited Vänijya and delivered a sermon. After listening to the sermon, Änand decided to follow Jainism by accepting the twelve vows of a householder. Änand observed these vows for fourteen years and progressed spiritually. One day Änand Shrävak attained a special ability known as Avadhi-jnän (clairvoyance) by performing severe penance, austerities, and meditation. His Avadhi-jnän was more pure and powerful than that acquired by other laypeople in their spiritual progress.

At this time Lord Mahävir and his disciples were in town. While returning from Gochari (getting food or alms), Gautam-swämi learned that many people were going to pay homage to Änand Shrävak for his newly acquired spiritual ability (Avadhi-jnän) and his austerities. He decided to visit him. Änand was

Gautam-swämi visiting Änand Shrävak

very happy to see Gautam-swämi, his guru (spiritual teacher). Though weak due to his austerities, he got up and welcomed Gautam-swämi warmly. Gautam-swämi inquired about his health and then asked about his new special ability. With due respect, Änand replied to Gautam-swämi, "Reverend Guru, I have attained a special ability (Avadhi-jnän) with which I can see as high as the first heaven and as low as the first hell."

Gautam-swämi explained to Änand, "A layman (Shrävak) can attain the special ability of Avadhi-jnän, but not of this magnitude. You need to do Präyashchitta (atonement) for imagining these visions." Änand was puzzled. He knew that he was correct but his Guru questioned his truthfulness and told him to repent for it. He therefore politely asked Gautam-swämi, "Does one need to repent for speaking the truth?" Gautam-swämi, equally puzzled, replied, "No one has to repent for speaking the truth." He then left Änand thinking that he would reconfirm this with Bhagawän Mahävir.

Gautam-swämi returned to Bhagawän Mahävir and asked about Änand's special ability. Mahävir replied, "Gautam, Änand was telling the truth. He has acquired Avadhi-jnän of such magnitude. Rarely does a layperson attain such power and knowledge. You should repent for your mistake." Gautam-swämi set aside his alms and immediately returned to Änand and asked for his forgiveness for doubting his honesty and truthfulness.

It is characteristic in Jain religion that if a Guru makes an error he should ask forgiveness from the disciple. Also if monks make an error then they should ask forgiveness from the laypeople.

In the later part of his life Änand fasted until death and then he was reborn as a heavenly being in Saudharma Devaloka (a heavenly region). After the completion of that heavenly life, he will be reborn as a human and will attain liberation.

The essence of human life is to practice one or more of the twelve vows in daily life. This story tells us how householders (Shrävaks) should have faith in truth. It also shows that Gautam-swämi was simple, humble and a true follower of Lord Mahävir. When Lord Mahävir pointed out his mistake, Gautam-swämi went to Änand without any hesitation, to ask for forgiveness even though he was the chief disciple of Mahävir-swämi. It also shows how impartial Lord Mahävir was because even though his chief disciple had made a mistake, he did not cover it up. On the contrary, he took the side of truth and explained his mistake to Gautam-swämi.

26 Puniä Shrävak

Puniä Shrävak and his wife were poor villagers by their own choice. They lived in a small hut made of mud and grass. Puniä had taken a vow not to earn more than the minimum needed to survive, which at that time was 12 Dokadas (1/12 of a rupee) a day, which he earned by spinning and selling cotton yarn. He had also taken another vow to offer food to virtuous people daily. As they could not afford to have more food to satisfy this vow, he would fast one day and his wife would fast the next day. In spite of their being so poor, they always offered their hospitality to fellow beings. In this way, the couple helped deserving people every day.

Puniä Shrävak did Sämäyika (48 minutes of meditation and equanimity) daily. Once during Sämäyika he could not meditate properly. He wondered what he had done that was disturbing his meditation but could not think of a reason. Therefore, he asked his wife, "What have we done different today that I cannot meditate properly?" At first his wife could not think of anything either. But as she continued thinking, she remembered that while returning from the market, she had picked up dry cow manure from the street and used that as cooking fire. She told Puniä about this. He told her that they should not take anything from anywhere unless it is bought from their own daily earnings. Even though dry cow manure lying on the street has no value and does not belong to anybody, they did not have the right to take it. Puniä could do a true Sämäyika because he lived a life of such high morals. Even Lord Mahävir praised his Sämäyika ritual in his sermon.

Once King Shrenik asked Lord Mahävir how he could destroy his bad Karmas to avoid being born in hell in his next life. He was ready to give up his entire kingdom for that. Lord Mahävir knew that it is not possible to change such Karma (birth Karma of the next life) once acquired by a person. However to convey this message properly to the King, he said, "If you can buy the Punya Karma of one Sämäyika from Puniä Shrävak then it may be possible to change the birth Karma of your next life."

King Shrenik's wealth is insignificant compared to the Sämäyika punya of Punia Shrävak

King Shrenik went to Puniä Shrävak and requested the Punya Karma of one of his Sämäyika. King Shrenik was ready to give his entire kingdom for this purchase. Puniä Shrävak said, "Sir, I do not need any money. You have given us all the things we need in our life. I am ready to give everything I possess including my life for you. You are a great and merciful king. However I do not know how to give my Sämäyika Punya to you. Good Karma cannot be purchased. One has to do good Karma personally."

King Shrenik asking for Sämäyika Punya from Punia Shrävak

Now King Shrenik realized that all his wealth could not buy Punya Karma of even one Sämäyika from a very poor man of his kingdom. King Shrenik left disappointed but with admiration for Puniä's real faith in religion.

This story shows that one can live a life of contentment even with limited earnings. We should not take anything that is not given to us. We should not accumulate more money than necessary to live. Vows or rituals are done for spiritual upliftment and not for monetary gain. To gain benefit from Sämäyika and other forms of meditation and penance, they should be motivated by one's inner self and not by any motives that conflict with Jain principles.

27 Shälibhadra

Once upon a time, there lived a poor woman and her son in a small village. One day, there was a festival in the village and all the kids, including the poor boy, were playing together. After playing, all except the poor boy, started to eat Kheer (rice pudding) that they had brought with them. The poor boy did not have Kheer to eat. He felt bad and ran home to his mother. He asked her if she would make some Kheer for him since all other children were eating it. His mother said that she could not make Kheer and told him to eat whatever she had cooked. He started crying and insisted on having Kheer. His mother could not bear to see him cry. Therefore, she went to a neighbor's house and borrowed some milk, sugar, and rice, and made Kheer for her son. She poured the Kheer into a dish and left to bring some water from the well.

As the boy was about to start eating, he heard the words, "Dharma Läbha" (meaning, may you be blessed with spirituality, usually spoken by Jain Sädhus and Sädhvis when they arrive at a lay person's house for Gochari - food). He saw a Jain Sädhu at the door. Without hesitation, the hungry boy invited the monk in and offered him the Kheer. He poured all the Kheer from his plate into the monk's container. He was happy that he could offer this to the monk even though nothing was left for him to eat. His good intentions and his pious action helped him earn good Karmas.

The boy is happily offering Kheer to the monk

In his next life he was born as Shälibhadra in a very rich family. His life was like being in heaven. His parents were Bhadrä Shethäni and Gobhadra Sheth. His father had renounced the world to become a monk when Shälibhadra was a young boy. His mother provided him all the comforts and luxury and never let him out of the palace for fear that he might become a monk like his father. It was said that even the heavenly beings were jealous of his lavish lifestyle. When he grew up, he was married to 32 beautiful women.

One day, some merchants from Nepal came to town to sell some very exquisite diamond studded shawls. They went to King Shrenik's court where the king told them that he could not afford to buy such expensive shawls. The merchants returned from court in utter disappointment because they were hoping to sell some shawls to the king. The merchants also thought that since the king could not afford to buy any then none of his people would have enough wealth to buy their shawls in this city and decided to leave town.

When Bhadrä Shethäni heard this, she sent a messenger and requested the merchants to visit her. The merchants were reluctant to go because if the king could not buy a shawl, how could any of the residents buy such expensive shawls! When they reached the house, Bhadrä Shethäni asked, "How many shawls do you have?" They said they had sixteen shawls. She said, "Only sixteen? I need thirty-two shawls because I have thirty-two daughters-in-law." The merchants thought she was joking believing that she would not even buy one. She said, "Please take out those shawls." They took out the sixteen shawls. The merchants were surprised that without a second thought she bought all sixteen shawls. They were further astounded to see her tearing such precious shawls into two pieces in front of them and giving a piece to each of her daughters-in-law to wipe their feet. The merchants were stunned but left with joy. The daughters-in-law used the pieces once and threw them away.

Bhadrä Shethäni buying very expensive shawls for her daughters-in-law

One of the servants at Shälibhadra's palace knew the queen so she took a piece of shawl for the queen. The queen was baffled but happy that such rich people lived in her kingdom. She told King Shrenik about the shawls and he was also very proud of such rich people upholding the good name of his kingdom. He invited Shälibhadra to his court to honor him. When Bhadrä Shethäni found out, she went to the king and told him that her son was very shy, and invited the king to come to their palace. King Shrenik accepted the invitation and went to Shälibhadra's palace. When King Shrenik reached there, he realized that his own palace was nothing compared to Shälibhadra's palace. Bhadrä Shethäni offered him a place to sit and asked Shälibhadra to come down to honor and respect the king.

Shälibhadra did not know anything about the king or his kingdom and thought that there was some sort of merchandise that his mother wanted to show him. So he said, "I do not want to see it but you go ahead and buy it." His mother said, "This is not merchandise. He is our king, our master, and you need to come down to greet and honor him." The word "master" started ringing in his ears. He wondered, "Why should I have a master over me? I should be the master of myself." While thinking like this, he came down and paid his respect to the king, but he did not stay very long.

He kept thinking that he was not a free person because there was someone like a king and master over him. He started to think about his father (who had become a monk) and the real meaning of life. He decided at that very moment to become a monk and told his family about his decision. His mother and all his wives tried to convince him to spend some more time with them. However, he was determined to renounce the world. Instead of renouncing all his possessions and family members at once, he agreed to spend one day with each of his wives and at the end of thirty-two days he would become a monk. He started to do that the very same day.

Shälibhadra had a sister named Subhadrä. She was married to Dhannä. Dhannä had eight wives. One day Subhadrä was giving her husband Dhannä a bath and suddenly tears rolled down her face and fell on him. He asked her why she was crying. She told him that her brother had decided to become a monk and that he had been spending one day with each of his wives and at the end of 32 days he will become a monk. Dhannä laughed and told Subhadrä, "Your brother is a coward. If he wants to become a monk, then why wait for 32 days?" Subhadrä was upset to hear that, and told her husband, "It is easier said than done." This sparked awareness in Dhannä's mind and he told her, "I am leaving all eight of you right now to become a monk." Subhadrä was taken by surprise. She thought that her husband was joking. However, Dhannä said, "It is too late now. I am determined to become a monk. If you all want to join me, you are welcome." Seeing Dhannä's determination, Subhadrä and his seven wives decided to become nuns.

Dhannä then went to his brother-in-law Shälibhadra's palace and challenged him, "Hey Shälibhadra! If you really want to leave your family and possessions, then what are you waiting for? Join me."

Shälibhadra heard him and accepted the challenge. He told his wives and other family members, "I am leaving you all today." He went down to join his brother-in-law. His wives joined him too. All of them went to Lord Mahävir, accepted Dikshä and became monks and nuns.

After observing severe penances as monks, Dhannä and Shälibhadra were born as heavenly beings in heaven. From there, they will be born again as human beings and attain liberation.

Selfless service always pays off. Neighbors helping neighbors reflects a caring society. The virtue of a charitable act in the life of a little boy was rewarded multiple times in the life of Shälibhadra. As a result, he was able to leave everything easily. Good deeds always leave an imprint on the soul. Good deeds and practicing penance ultimately leads to the liberation of the soul.

28 King Shrenik and Queen Chelnä

This is a story from the time of Bhagawän Mahävir. At that time, King Chetak was the ruler of Vaishäli. He had a beautiful daughter named Chelnä. Once an artist painted a picture of Chelnä and showed it to King Shrenik of Magadha. Charmed by Chelnä's beauty, Shrenik fell in love with her. One day Chelnä came to the city of Magadha where she saw king Shrenik and she too fell in love with him. They soon got married.

Queen Chelnä was a devoted follower of Jainism, while Shrenik was influenced by Buddhism. The king was very generous and had a big heart, but somehow he was not happy with his queen's devotion to Jain monks. He wanted to prove to Chelnä that Jain monks were pretenders. He strongly believed that Jain monks could not follow the practice of self-restraint and non-violence to the extent that Jain philosophy claims, and that the equanimity shown by Jain monks was superficial. Chelnä was greatly disturbed by this.

King Shrenik testing a Jain monk's equanimity

One day King Shrenik went on a hunting trip where he saw a Jain monk, Yamadhar, engaged in deep meditation. Shrenik let his hunting dogs go after Yamadhar but the monk remained silent and in deep meditation. On seeing the calmness and composure of the monk, the dogs became quiet. King Shrenik got angry and thought that the monk had played some trick on them. Therefore, he started shooting arrows at the monk, but they kept missing him. Becoming more upset, he finally put a dead snake around Yamadhar's neck and returned to his palace.

The king narrated the whole incident to his queen Chelnä. The queen felt very sorry for Yamadhar and took the king back to Yamadhar's place of meditation. Because of the dead snake, ants and other insects were crawling all over the monk's body, but the monk did not even stir. The couple witnessed the limits of human endurance. The queen gently removed the ants and the snake from the monk's body and cleaned his wounds. She applied sandalwood paste. Sometime later Yamadhar opened his eyes and blessed both of them.

Jain monk enduring pain while in meditation

The monk did not distinguish between the king who had caused him pain and the queen who had alleviated his pain. King Shrenik was very impressed and became convinced that Jain monks were truly free from attachment and aversion. Thus, King Shrenik along with queen Chelnä became devoted to Jainism and Bhagawän Mahävir.

If one cannot perform a comparable level of penance and devotion, one should not doubt the willpower and devotion of someone who is more religious. In fact, one should be very respectful of such individuals. It is important to serve and support these people rather than cause them pain and suffering. This will help to avoid the accumulation of bad Karma. Learn to accept and appreciate virtues in others.

29 Abhaykumär and Thief Rohineya

During the time of Lord Mahävir there was a burglar named Lohkhur. He lived in a remote cave in the Vaibhärgiri hill near the city of Räjgrihi. He was very clever in his profession and never left any traces of his burglary. He and his wife, Rohini, had a son named Rohineya. As Rohineya grew up, he learned his father's profession and eventually became an expert burglar. He even surpassed his father in intelligence and smartness. It was almost impossible to recognize him when he was in disguise. If someone pursued him, he could outrun him or her. He robbed the rich and hid the treasures in the most unexpected and inaccessible places. He extended help to the poor from the wealth that he accumulated. Many of them felt grateful and were pleased with him. Therefore, they were not willing to help government officials to track him down.

Lohkhur was now very old and could see that his life was coming to an end. When he was on his deathbed, he called Rohineya and said that he was very happy with the expertise that he had shown in committing burglary, their ancestral profession. In order to remain successful, he advised his son never to listen to the sermons of Lord Mahävir because his teachings were not conducive to their profession. Rohineya promised his father he would abide by his advice.

After Lohkhur died, Rohineya expanded his burglary so much that it became almost impossible for rich families to ensure the safety of their property when they went out. They were constantly afraid that Rohineya would go to their home during their absence and take the jewelry and other valuables. Some people went to King Shrenik and requested him to take action to protect them from Rohineya's burglaries, since police officers had failed to do anything about the matter. The king therefore asked his most intelligent chief minister Abhaykumär to take charge of arresting Rohineya.

Once, while Rohineya was secretly on his way to Räjgrihi, he had to pass by the side of the Lord Mahävir's assembly hall. He remembered his father's advice not to ever listen to Lord Mahävir's sermon. He put his hands over his ears. Unfortunately, at that moment he stepped on a sharp thorn that went deep into his foot. He had to take his hands off his ears in order to take out the thorn. During this time, he heard the following words:

> ***'Human life is the best of all lives. It is possible to attain liberation only as a human. Every human being can attain salvation irrespective of caste, creed, or color. By virtuous deeds, one can gain a life in heaven where all sorts of pleasures and happiness exists.'***

When heavenly beings walk their feet do not touch the ground. Their bodies are without shadow, their eyes remain steady, and their garlands do not wither. However, the life of a heavenly being does not lead to ultimate liberation, which provides eternal bliss and happiness. Therefore, heavenly beings crave a human life.'

By that time Rohineya had removed the thorn from his foot and covering his ears again with his hands, he proceeded towards the city.

Thief Rohineya accidentally hears a sermon given by Bhagawän Mahävir

In the city, Abhaykumär had secretly posted trained soldiers in disguise at the gates and at all important locations. He himself remained watchful. When Rohineya entered the city, a trained soldier recognized him even though he was in the disguise of a farmer. The soldier sent a message to Abhaykumär that an unidentified person had entered the city. Abhaykumär became very alert. As Rohineya passed by, Abhaykumär glanced at him from a secret place. He recognized the burglar even in disguise and instructed his men to surround him. Smart as Rohineya was, he quickly recognized the danger. He ran towards the city wall. Unfortunately for him, there were soldiers near the wall. He was thus easily apprehended and was put in jail.

The next day he was presented in the royal court. As Rohineya was in disguise, it was hard to identify him as the burglar. Abhaykumär was of course sure but how could the accused be punished without proof of his identity? When the king asked him about his identity, Rohineya replied that he was a farmer named Durgachandra and belonged to the Shäligräm village. He had come to Räjgrihi to visit the capital and was returning home when the watchmen apprehended him. Rohineya had made arrangements for that assumed identity with the residents of the village. When inquiries were made in that village, the people confirmed what Rohineya had stated in court.

Abhaykumär had to devise a plan for getting a confession from Rohineya regarding the burglaries. He came to know that Rohineya was fond of drinks. He therefore arranged to serve an excessive amount of wine to the thief. The excessive wine made him unconscious. While unconscious, Rohineya was cleaned, dressed in extravagantly perfumed royal garments, and adorned with valuable jewelry. He was then placed on a luxurious velvet bed of sandalwood on the top floor of a palatial building. As Rohineya regained his consciousness, he saw himself in heavenly surroundings. There was a breathtaking view all around: the walls, ceiling and floor were crystalline, beautiful maidens were waving scented air with diamond studded fans, soft serene music was heard in the background, and fairylike dancers were dancing in tune with the music, and divine musicians were getting ready for a musical concert.

Rohineya could not make out where he was. He asked one of the girls where he was and why all of them were serving him so well. The girl replied that he was their new king in heaven. He had attained all the divine comforts, which now belonged to him. He could live like Indra, the king of heaven, and enjoy life with heavenly damsels.

'Could this be true for a burglar like me?' he asked himself. However, he then remembered that he was helpful to the poor and needy, and he was sure that God had been just. 'Or could this be the plan of Abhaykumär?' he thought again. It was hard for him to decide what the truth really was. He therefore thought it was best to wait and see.

Make-believe heaven created by Abhaykumär

After a while, a luxuriously clad person entered with a golden staff and a book in his hand. 'Is your new Lord awake?' he asked one of the damsels. The girl replied that their new Lord had just woken up and that they were getting ready to celebrate his arrival in heaven by presenting the divine concert. 'Let me make sure that all preparations pertaining to his arrival have been completed before you start your concert; and let me also get some information from him that the heavenly realm needs to know.' As he was saying this, he came to Rohineya. Opening his book, he asked Rohineya to narrate his deeds from his previous life prior to enjoying the amenities of heaven.

Meanwhile, Rohineya was looking around. He remembered what he had heard from Lord Mahävir's sermon about heavenly beings, when he stepped on the thorn. He observed the movements of heavenly beings in front of him. He noticed that their feet were touching the ground, their bodies had shadows, and their eyes were blinking like human beings. He immediately figured out that this heaven was not real and was only an illusion created by Abhaykumär to gain evidence of his burglaries.

He therefore replied that in the previous life he had given donations to worthy causes, had constructed temples, had been on pilgrimages to holy places and had rendered service to deserving people. The person took note of his statement and asked him to narrate any wrong deeds that he might have indulged in. Rohineya said that he had scrupulously avoided misdeeds and therefore he was born in heaven. Abhaykumär's plan did not work and Rohineya was set free as being the innocent farmer that he pretended to be.

Rohineya was released, but he constantly thought about what had happened. He realized that what he had accidentally heard from Lord Mahävir had saved his life. Then how could his father be right in the advice that he had given? Lord Mahävir must be a very great entity. 'If those words which were accidentally heard were so helpful, imagine how helpful his teachings would be?' he asked himself. Had he wasted his years avoiding the sermons of the Lord? After pondering at length, he decided to go to Lord Mahävir and to serve at his feet. He went to the assembly and humbly requested the Lord to accept him as his disciple. He also requested to become a monk. Mahävir asked him to disclose his real identity and confess all his past sins to the king before renouncing his worldly life.

He then disclosed his real identity to the king who was present in the assembly and was ready to accept any punishment. He also requested Abhaykumär to accept all the treasures he had collected during his burglaries.

Since Rohineya had voluntarily confessed and had willingly returned everything that he had taken, the king decided to pardon him and permitted him to become a monk. Rohineya deeply repented for what he had done in his life. He started observing severe austerities in order to erase the Karmas acquired by his misdeeds. In his old age, with permission from Lord Mahävir, he adopted Sanlekhanä (avoiding food and staying in meditation until death). After his death he was born in heaven.

The theme here focuses on honesty and the principle of non-stealing. One should not steal from others even if one intends to donate the stolen items to the poor. Wrongdoing is still wrongdoing regardless of how much good you are doing in other areas. One must repent in order to destroy the bad Karmas that accumulate as a result of wrongdoing.

The second thing we learn from this story is that we can attain liberation only through the human form. Even heavenly beings cannot attain liberation without being born as human beings. So we should realize how fortunate we are to have this human birth, and we should make the most of it and wash away as many bad Karma as we can. Also, look at the power of Lord Mahävir's sermon. Just a few words from his sermon saved and then ultimately changed Rohineya's life forever. Imagine the benefit of listening to all His teachings. Unfortunately, we cannot listen to His sermons directly, but we have his teachings available to us as Ägams. We should study and understand the Ägams as much as we can so that our lives can change for the better just like that of Rohineya.

Part V
Stories after Bhagawän Mahävir

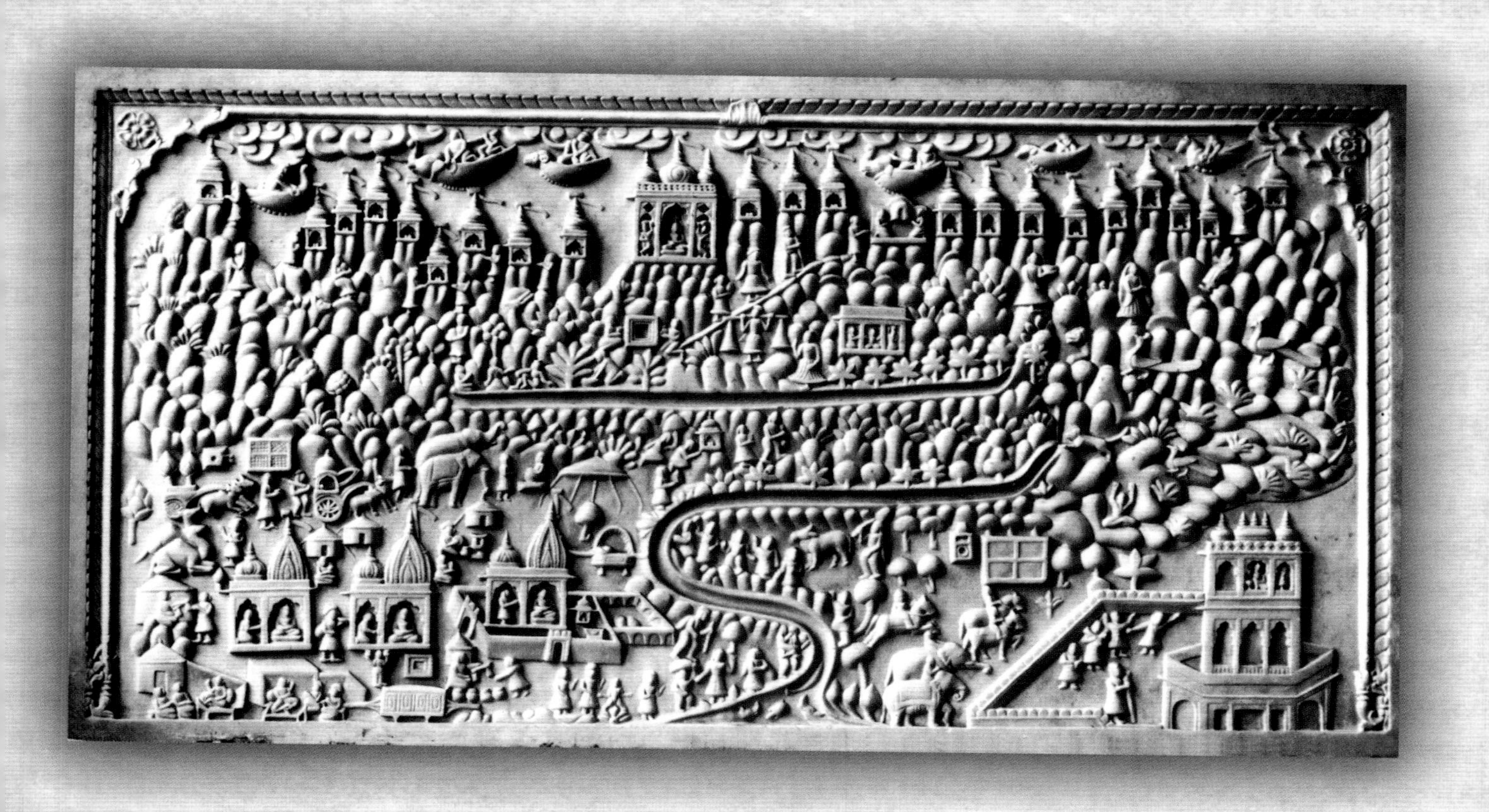

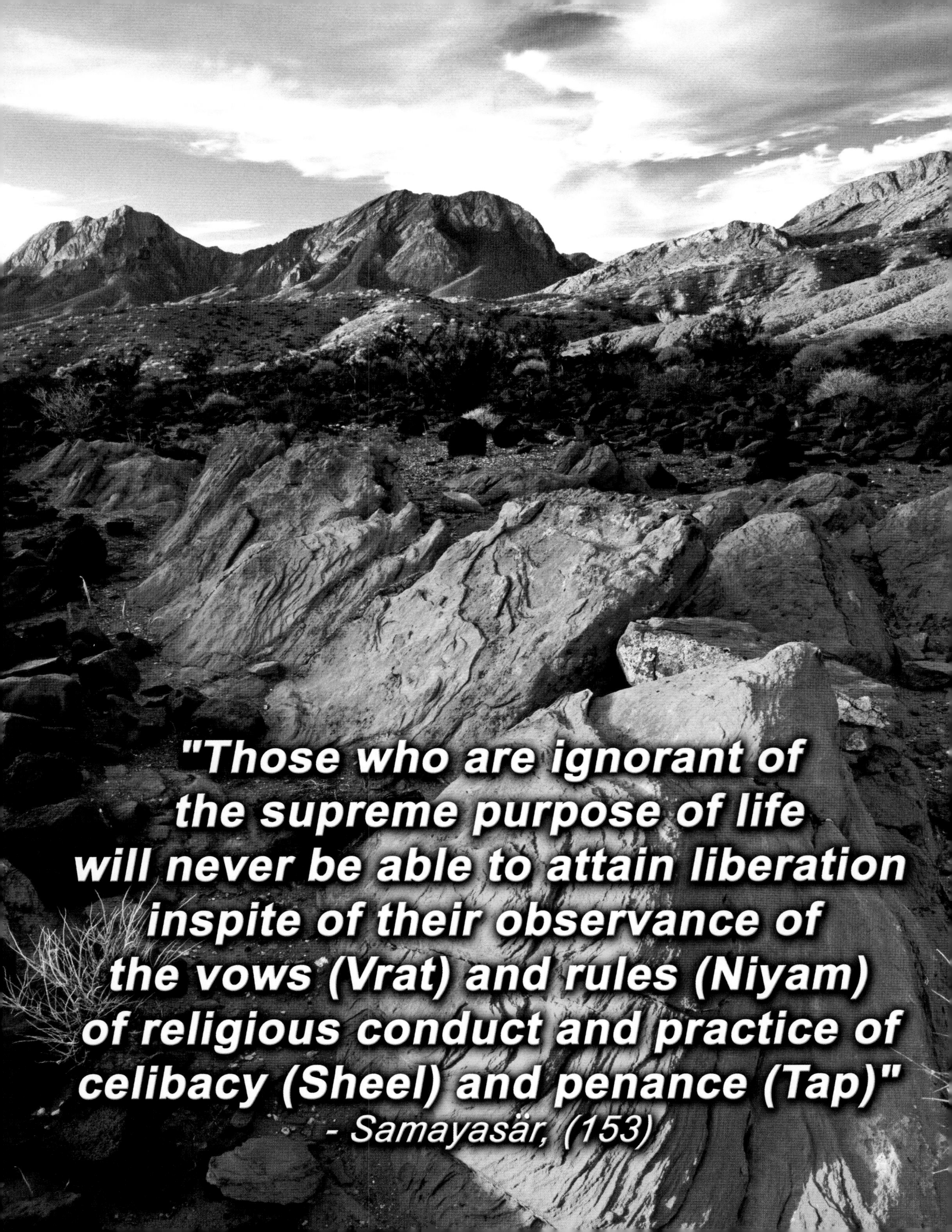
"Those who are ignorant of
the supreme purpose of life
will never be able to attain liberation
inspite of their observance of
the vows (Vrat) and rules (Niyam)
of religious conduct and practice of
celibacy (Sheel) and penance (Tap)"
- Samayasär, (153)

30 Vajrakumär

In the city of Tumbivan, there lived a rich Brahmin called Dhangiri. He had a beautiful wife named Sunandä. Their life was full of joy. When Sunandä was pregnant, she had a beautiful dream. She told her husband, who was also a scholar, about the dream. He told her that she would give birth to a bright and charming child. She felt very happy.

One day a Jain Ächärya named Sinhgiri came to the city. Both Dhangiri and Sunandä went to listen to his sermons regularly. Dhangiri's soul was awakened by these sermons, and he lost interest in his wealth, family, and worldly affairs. He decided to give up his worldly life and become a monk. He told his wife about his decision. She was shocked. She tried to convince him to stay and enjoy their life together. She also said that since they were going to have a child, it would be better to stay together to raise the child. Dhangiri did not change his mind. Nonetheless, he made the necessary financial arrangement for his family. Sunandä, who was the daughter of a religious merchant Dhanpäl, had a deep understanding of religion. Therefore, she accepted his decision. Sunandä was consoled that at least she was the wife of a virtuous man.

A few months later, Sunandä gave birth to a very handsome boy. He was lovable because he always had a smile on his face. Everybody who saw him liked him from the very first glance. Sunandä celebrated his birth. She felt happy that she had a son to raise but her happiness did not last long. One day some ladies from the neighborhood were visiting her and started talking about her husband. One of them said, "If Dhangiri had not taken Dikshä (to become a monk), then he would have celebrated the birth with more extravagance than Sunandä." The child, although a baby, heard the word "Dikshä" and started thinking. He felt as if he had heard the word Dikshä before. While thinking about it, he suddenly remembered his past life. He realized that he was on the right spiritual path. He decided that he should take advantage of being born as a human again and should utilize this life to further uplift his soul. He should become a monk like his father. He also realized that his mother would not let him go because he was her only hope and joy. He started thinking about what could be done to get her permission.

At last, he came to the decision that since his mother would not let him go willingly; he should create a situation whereby she might get tired of him and give him up. He was still a little boy in the crib when he thought, "If I keep crying all the time then she will get tired of me and maybe she will try to get rid of me." He put his thoughts to work right away. He started crying. His mother came running to comfort him, but he just kept crying. She tried everything but nothing helped to quiet him down. She took him to the doctors and took advice from others but nothing worked. The child's trick worked. Even their neighbors who had liked this child very much got tired of him. Finally, his mother was fed up with him but did not know what to do with him. The child was now six months old and monk Dhangiri (the child's father) and Ächärya Sinhgiri visited the city again. Sunandä came to know about this and thought of giving the child to his father.

At the usual time for alms (going to collect food), Dhangiri Muni asked permission from the Ächärya to go for alms. Ächärya Sinhgiri told him, "Dhangiri, today you may accept even a live thing if it is offered." The Ächärya possessed a special power and he knew what alms monk Dhangiri was going to get so he gave his permission ahead of time. Although Muni Dhangiri did not understand what his guru meant, he left for alms. On his route to various houses, he arrived at Sunandä's house. He said, "Dharma Läbha"

(May you follow the proper religion). Sunandä recognized the voice. She welcomed Muni Dhangiri and expressed happiness in seeing him again. She invited him to enter the house for food.

The young boy also heard Muni Dhangiri's words "Dharma Läbha". He thought that this was the best opportunity for his trick so he started crying. This irritated his mother and she told the monk, "You are lucky to be able to uplift your soul but I am tired with the burden of your child. He does nothing but cry. He does not let me rest and I am very unhappy. Please accept him so there will be peace in the house." The child heard these words and became very happy in his mind. He hoped that Muni would accept her proposal. Muni Dhangiri remembered the words of his Guru spoken right before he left for alms. Now he understood what his Guru meant. He said, "Sunandä, if you really want to give this child away, I will accept him, but please think twice. Once you give him away you will not be able to get him back. You will have no right to this child after that." On hearing this, the child started crying even louder. She said, "I do not want to hear this crying anymore. I am so sick and tired of him that I do not want him around at all. You can take him forever."

She picked up the child and put him in the Muni's cloth bag. As soon as the boy was handed over to the Muni, he stopped crying and started smiling. Sunandä was surprised by this and kept looking at the boy. However, she was determined to give him away. Muni left with the child to go to the Upäshray (place where monks stay). Ächärya Sinhgiri saw that Muni Dhangiri was carrying something heavy. So he asked him, "Why is your bag so heavy?" When the Muni opened his bag, his Guru saw the handsome smiling boy. Since he was so heavy the Ächärya named him "Vajrakumär".

Ächärya Sinhgiri requested a prominent Jain Shrävak (householder) to take care of Vajrakumär and to make sure that he was taught Jain religious teachings as he had the potential of being a great Ächärya in the future. The Shrävak brought Vajrakumär home and told his wife what Ächärya Sinhgiri wanted them to do. She was a very religious woman and happily agreed to the wishes of the Ächärya. She loved the boy so much that she would not let him go anywhere without her. She always took him to the Upäshray to see the Sädhvis (nuns). Even though he was little, he listened to and memorized all the scriptures the nuns were reciting. By the time, he was three years old, he had learned up to eleven Angas (oldest Jain scriptures). He was respectful to everybody and talked very intelligently.

One day, one of Sunandä's friends came to her house and said, "Do you know that your child, who kept crying, spends a lot of his time at our Upäshray? I have never heard him cry. He is a very charming and lovable child." Sunandä tried to ignore what her friends told her but after all she was Vajrakumär's mother. She longed to see her son again. She started thinking, "How could I have done such a terrible thing? How could I have given up my precious child to a Muni? After all, he is my child. I should get him back."

A few days later, Ächärya Sinhgiri and Muni Dhangiri came to Tumbivan again. She went to the Upäshray. She approached Muni Dhangiri and asked him "Please, give my son back. I cannot live without him any more." Muni Dhangiri said, "I told you at that time that once you have given him away you will not get him back. Remember, you said you did not want him at all. We cannot give back what we take."

Sunandä said, "I do not know why I did that. I cannot live without my son. Please find a way to give me back my son."

Ächärya Sinhgiri and Muni Dhangiri tried to convince her to forget him, but she was determined to get him back.

At last, she went to the king and requested, "Please help me get my son back. My husband has become a monk and I am lonely. He is the only child I have. Please ask them to return my son."

The king heard the whole story from Sunandä. He said, "Let me find out what happened, and I will let you know shortly." He inquired about the situation and found that because Sunandä was tired of her son's incessant crying, she had voluntarily given away her child.

The king called Sunandä and told her, "Sunandä, when Muni Dhangiri came to your house for alms you gave your child away voluntarily because you were fed up with his crying. Once you give something you cannot have it back."

Sunandä said, "Oh King, this is not a thing. This is my own flesh and blood, and he is the only hope I have. Please do something to get him back. I cannot live without him."

The king could feel the motherly affection and sincerity in her voice. He was also puzzled. Ultimately he told Sunandä, "I will call you and Muni Dhangiri in the courthouse and let Vajrakumär decide whom he wants to go with. Is it okay with you?"

Sunandä said, "Yes, Your Majesty."

Sunandä offering her child to Muni Dhangiri

The next day, the king's courthouse was full of people curious to see what would happen to the child. Sunandä came with toys, sweets, clothes, and other novelty items to attract Vajrakumär. The king and all his ministers came. Muni Dhangiri came with other monks. Everybody in the courthouse including the king paid homage to the monks. Vajrakumär also came.

The king told Vajrakumär, "Vajrakumär, although you are very little, you are a very intelligent boy." Pointing towards his mother, he said, "She is your mother. She is very affectionate and loving. She has lots of toys, sweets, and good clothes for you. She wants you back. On the other side," pointing towards Monk Dhangiri, he continued, "there is a Monk who has given up worldly life. He is full of restraint and lives the life of renunciation. He is very virtuous and a revered person. He also wants to keep you with him to teach you about spiritual life. Now you must decide which way you want to go. Do you want to go with your mother or with the monk?"

There was pin drop silence. Everybody was eagerly waiting to see what Vajrakumär would decide. Vajrakumär was very serious today. He got up, and as he walked, he glanced at his mother and Muni Dhangiri. Sunandä started screaming, "Son, come here. See, I have brought you toys, sweets, and new clothes. Please, please, come to me."

On the other side, Muni Dhangiri did not have anything with him except an Ogho (a broom to clean the way before walking). He showed that to Vajrakumär.

Vajrakumär picked up the Ogho and started dancing with it. He started smiling again. Then he decided to sit down with Muni Dhangiri and looked at everybody with a joyful face.

Everybody in the courthouse, including the king and Sunandä, were amazed that the young boy decided on monkhood instead of a luxurious worldly life. Sunandä accepted the decision of Vajrakumär and wished him success. She celebrated Vajrakumär's dikshä with joy and delight. Later, Vajrakumär became a great Ächärya.

A human soul is capable of having high religious values and faith at any age. The story of Vajrakumär clearly shows us that it is never too early to learn religious values and to practice religion.

31 King Samprati

King Samprati was a great Jain king who lived during the second half of the third and the first half of the second century BC. He was the grandson of the great king Ashok and the son of king Kunäl.

Jain history provides some details of his life. Buddhist literature also mentions him by the Präkrit name Sampadi. His name occurs in some of the Hindu Puräns, wherein he is variously referred to as Samprati, Sampati, and Saptati, etc. Moreover, coins depicting a crescent and bearing his name have now been found. The sign of the crescent represents the Jain symbol of Siddhashilä and the three dots are symbolic of the Jain trio of Right Faith, Right Knowledge and Right Conduct. Some of the coins also show a Swastika below the three dots. This is conclusive evidence of him being a Jain king.

Samprati was raised and educated in Avanti and became the king of Avanti in 232 BC. While he was prince, he once saw a grand Jain procession led by Ächärya Suhastigiri, who was the head of the Jain religious order. On seeing the Ächärya, Samprati felt that he had seen him somewhere. While deeply pondering over it, he faintly remembered that the Ächärya was his Guru in an earlier life. Samprati bowed to the Ächärya and asked whether he knew him. The Ächärya thought for a while and remembered that Samprati was his disciple in the previous life.

Various incidences in King Samprati's life

There was a severe famine when Ächärya Suhastigiri was in the city of Kaushämbi. During the famine it was very difficult for Jain monks to get alms. Jain householders, however, made sure that the monks received alms. At that time, there was a poor man who could hardly get any food and was starving. He noticed that the monks were getting enough food even during the severe famine. Therefore, he requested the Ächärya to give him some food. Foreseeing that the man had great potential to be a great Jain legend in the next birth, the Ächärya told him that he could get food if he became a monk.

The man gladly agreed. Accordingly, he was initiated and thereby received enough food to eat. Since he had been starving for many days, he ate too much. Consequently, he had severe stomach pains, which he endured patiently while cursing himself for eating too much. Other monks served him in all possible ways, but the pain did not subside. On the contrary, it continued to become worse and the newly initiated monk died of the pain that very night. Due to his adopting the restraints of monkhood and bearing the pain quietly, he was reborn as the grandson of the great King Ashok.

The Ächärya narrated the entire episode to him. Samprati was glad to hear that. He realized the benefits of adopting Jainism even for a short while. He adopted it as his faith and formally accepted the Ächärya as his Guru. After he became a king, he offered his kingdom to the Guru because it was obtained on account of his benevolence. The Ächärya, however, declined to accept it and said that as a Jain monk he did not want to possess anything. He pointed out that Samprati should try his best to promote and encourage Jainism in his kingdom and beyond.

Samprati accepted the advice. He became a devout Jain and followed Jain principles. He was a brave king and expanded his kingdom considerably in the South up to the Vindhya Mountains, and in the West to the Arabian Sea. He constructed many Jain temples, not only in his dominion, but also encouraged the rulers of Andhra Pradesha, Karnatak, and Maharashtra to do so. Jain tradition indicates that during his lifetime he arranged for the installation of more than 100,000 Tirthankar idols and for the construction or renovation of 36,000 temples. He also sent his missionaries abroad to Afghanistan, Nepal, Sri Lanka, Burma and even China to spread the message of Jainism. It is hardly surprising that in the 'Early History of India' Vincent Smith calls Samprati the Jain Ashok, as king Ashok is known for spreading Buddhism.

He treated other followers of Jainism very affectionately and helped them in every way. Since he vividly remembered his starvation in his previous life, he was sympathetic to all poor people and took care to see that they did not starve. He set up 700 charitable dharamshäläs where anyone could eat free of charge.

Samprati had no children. He took this as the consequence of his earlier Karma and observed the religious customs scrupulously. After ruling over his large kingdom for 53 years, he died in 179 BC. Jain tradition believes that he was reborn as a heavenly being.

Service to others is one of the many ways one can follow Jainism, and Samprati certainly demonstrated this quality. He not only helped promote Jainism by renovating and building temples and installing Tirthankar idols in existing temples, but he also helped reduce the pain and suffering of the poor. We should also strive to serve others. His life story demonstrates that a religious deed performed even for a short while gives manifold results. In addition, it creates a chain of good deeds leading to beneficial results.

32 Temples of Delwädä

Mount Abu is a beautiful town on a mountain top in the state of Rajasthan. Within the town, there are two magnificent Jain temples known as the Delwädä Temples. The carvings in both these temples are breathtaking. The carvings in the marble ceilings of these temples are so minute and intricate that it is difficult to copy the design even on a piece of paper. These temples are regarded as 'poetry in marble'.

Vimalshä built the first temple in the 11th Century AD at a cost of 180 million Rupees. The second temple, called Lunig Vasahi, was built by two brothers – Vastupäl and Tejpäl, in the memory of their elder brother, in the 13th Century AD, at a cost of 120 million Rupees. The stories associated with the architects of these two temples are presented here.

Vimalshä

The Solanki dynasty was the golden period for the state of Gujarat, India, when the authority and prosperity of the state reached its peak. The credit for putting Gujarat in this position mainly goes to the king's chancellors and commanders who were at the helm of affairs. It is interesting to know that many of the chancellors and some of the commanders of that period were Jains. Vimalshä was a very capable and outstanding commander in several respects.

King Mulräj, the founder of the Solanki dynasty, had an advisor named Vir Mahattam. His wife's name was Virmati. They had three sons named Nedh, Vimal, and Chahil. While they were still very young, their father renounced worldly life and became a monk. Their mother then went to her parents' place and raised her sons with love and care. Nedh was very intelligent and grew up to be a wise, considerate youth. Vimal was bold and smart. He liked horseback riding and archery. He steadily gained expertise in those arts and in due course turned out to be a well known equestrian and an accomplished archer.

As the sons grew older, their mother brought them back to the capital city of Pätan so that they could pursue a career of their choice. In line with their interests, Nedh joined the royal court and Vimal joined the army. Both of them quickly began to rise in the ranks and became known for their outstanding capabilities. Since Vimal in particular was handsome and brave, he impressed a multimillionaire of Pätan who had a beautiful daughter named Shridevi. He thought Vimal would be a perfect husband for his daughter. Vimal agreed, and Shridevi and Vimal got married

Luck continued to favor both the brothers. During the reign of King Bhimdev who came to the throne in 1021 AD, Nedh became the chancellor and Vimal secured the position of commander. Vimal was thus fortunate to get a beautiful, loving wife and a high ranking military position at a relatively young age. Moreover, because of his amicable nature, he soon won the hearts of everyone and came to be known as Vimalshä.

Some people at the court could not bear the good fortune of Vimalshä. They were jealous and began to look for his drawbacks. They noticed that Vimalshä would not bow to anyone, not even the king, before offering obeisance to the omniscient Jain Tirthankars. Thereupon, they started telling King Bhimdev that Vimalshä was arrogant due to his position and was not even willing to bow to the king. They said his ambition knew no bounds and he might even try to acquire the throne. Unfortunately, Bhimdev started to believe those courtiers and began to look at Vimalshä with suspicion.

When Vimalshä learned of the disaffection of King Bhimdev, he decided to leave Pätan. Accordingly, he went to mount Abu (which was known as Chandraväti at that time) with his followers. There he learned that Dhandhuk, the chief of Chandraväti, was aspiring to become independent from the sovereign King Bhimdev. Vimalshä attacked him with the force at his command. Dhandhuk could not fight him and fled. Vimalshä thus occupied Chandraväti. He had no ambition to become the king and took possession of Chandraväti in the name of King Bhimdev and considered himself the governor of the place.

Vimalshä was now happily passing his days at Chandraväti with his wife. Shridevi was a very affectionate lady and made him happy in every respect. They had no children. Being religious minded, however, the couple considered it as the consequence of their unwholesome Karma. Once they happened to meet Dharmaghosh-suri, who was the well known Jain Ächärya of that time. Vimalshä regularly listened to his sermons which made him even more religiously oriented.

As he remembered his involvement in past wars, he felt very sorry for the violence and sins he had committed. He sincerely repented for it. In view of his genuine repentance, the Ächärya asked him to construct a temple at Chandraväti and make it a center of pilgrimage to help atone for the violence caused during the wars. Vimalshä was pleased to hear this suggestion and made up his mind to construct a grand temple.

He was also a devotee of Ambikä Devi, the goddess in service of Tirthankar Neminäth. He decided to invoke her in order to get her blessings. The goddess was pleased with the earnestness of his worship and asked him what he wanted. He asked for a son and the capability to construct a monumental temple at Chandraväti. However, the goddess asked him to select one of the two. Vimalshä opted for the temple. Goddess Ambikä granted his wish.

Then Vimalshä selected a site for the temple on top of a mountain and bought the land for 45,360,000 gold coins. The foundation stone was laid with deep faith. However, it was not easy to construct the temple. It was a Herculean task. Artisans were not locally available, there was no road leading from the foot of the mountain to the top, and marble had to be brought from a great distance. Vimalshä was determined to complete the project at any cost. He made all the necessary arrangements for transporting the materials to the top and hired the best sculptors in the country for carrying out the work.

All possible care was taken to see that the artisans did not face any difficulty, and the project did not encounter any problems. It took 14 years to finish the project and the temple was constructed at a cost of 185,300,000 gold coins. The opening ceremony was performed with great fanfare and enthusiasm under the guidance of Dharmaghosh-suri, Vardhamänsuri, and other Ächäryas.

Intricate carving in the ceiling of Delwädä Temple

It is a spacious, all marble temple. There are highly artistic figures in its domes, arcs, and panels. The sculptures are exquisite. It would be nearly impossible to bring out that sort of accuracy even in wax. The fact that the artists have done it in marble is marvelous and draws the instantaneous admiration of every visitor. These types of sculpture are not found anywhere else in the world. It is said that Vimalshä paid the artists in gold – the artisans collected the marble dust that they had carved for the day and brought it in and had it weighed. The person in charge would give them gold equal to the weight of stone powder! His generosity and the beauty of the temple have immortalized his name. It is virtually a wonder of the world. Later on, Vimalshä led a Jain Sangha to Shatrunjay Mountain located in the town of Palitana that cost 40 million gold coins. He constructed the Vimalvasahi temple there. It is located on the way to the main complex on the hill. It is a small but equally exquisite temple. It is popularly known as Bhulbhulämani temple, meaning a maze temple. He also constructed the well-known temples of Kumbhäriä on the Äräsur hill on the northern border of Gujarat. Moreover, he is credited with the construction of a beautiful temple in the capital city of Pätan.

Shridevi and Viamalshä praying to Goddess Ambikä

One successful but highly instructive anecdote is associated with his later life. It is said that Shridevi had a dream in which she saw a goddess. The goddess asked her to go to the temple along with her husband at midnight on a specific date and ask for whatever they wanted. Both of them were eager to have a son and went to the temple to express their wish. While they were waiting for midnight to arrive, they felt thirsty. Vimalshä therefore went to an adjoining well to fetch water. Inside the well there were steps which went all the way down to the water level. While he was going down the steps to get the water, someone asked him to pay toll for taking water. Vimalshä was amazed to hear that and asked the person why he was demanding toll to drink the water. The person replied that he was a descendent of the person who had built the well. Since he was poor, he was collecting a toll for using the well.

Vimalshä was taken aback to hear that. He asked himself, "What would happen if one day some of my own descendents tried to collect a toll for the temple that I have built?" He shuddered at the idea and again asked himself whether it would be better in that case to remain without a child. He went up and told his wife about the incident. She concurred with his thinking. At midnight when the goddess asked them what they wanted, Shridevi replied that she did not want a child anymore. Now, it was the turn of the goddess to be taken aback. Vimalshä narrated what he had experienced and said that they wanted to remain childless.

Vastupäl and Tejpäl

Two brothers, Vastupäl and Tejpäl were ministers in the court of King Vir-Dhaval in Gujarat. Tejpäl was also a very outstanding commander of the army. Both brothers made their name by their valor and faithfulness. They helped the king to conquer enemies and maintain law and order in the kingdom. Tejpäl's wife Anupamä-devi was a wise and smart woman, who always helped her husband in family matters. She was sweet spoken and a very religious and compassionate woman.

Tejpäl had always respected her opinion. Once, the families of both the brothers and many others went on a pilgrimage. They came to a small village. This particular area was not regarded as very safe for the pilgrims because the road was frequented by dacoits. Thinking that they might meet some dacoits on the way, the brothers decided to bury and hide their wealth in the nearby area. They started digging a hole but to their amazement, they unearthed a big pot of jewels and coins from the ground. They simply did not know what to do with this wealth.

Tejpäl asked Anupamä-devi what they should do with this immense wealth. Anupamä-devi had no hesitation in replying that this wealth had come from a deep trench but the right place for it was on a high mountain. This would spread the glory of Jainism. Thus, they decided to take it to the top of the mountain and spend it there.

The brothers decided to build a temple on Mt. Abu. It is known as Lunig Vasahi Temple. Tirthankar Neminäth Bhagawän's Samavasaran has also been carved in this temple. Tejpäl had also dedicated two Gokhlas (niches) for two women, one to commemorate his wife and the other to commemorate his brother's wife (sister-in-law). These niches are called 'Deräni-Jethäni nä Gokhlas' (The wives of two brothers are known as Deräni – Jethäni. Deräni is the younger one and Jethäni is the older brother's wife).

They constructed many more temples of which only the Delwädä temple and the Neminäth Temple of Mount Girnar exist today. However, the Lunig Vasahi Temple of Mount Abu is similar to that of the Vimalshä Temple. Fifty-two Deva Kulikas (subsidiary shrines) have also been constructed on an elevated platform around the central temple, each with the statue of a Tirthankar. Elephants were used to carry the marble to Mount Abu for the construction of the temples. A place called Hasti Shälä is also built within the temple complex to commemorate the contribution of elephants.

The contribution made by Vimalshä, Vastupäl and Tejpäl to the architecture of Jain temples is very inspiring. Their dedication to their religion, and their perseverance and honesty are praiseworthy. Their contribution to Jain architecture is part of our great heritage.

33 Udayan Mantri and His Sons - Ämbad and Bähad

Udayan Mantri (Minister)

The Solanki dynasty was the golden period for the state of Gujarat and the prosperity of the State reached its peak during the reign of King Kumärpäl. The credit for attaining this position mainly goes to his chancellors who were known as Mantris. It is interesting to learn that many of the chancellors of the Solanki period were Jains. The contribution of Udayan Mantri and his sons Ämbad and Bähad to the rise and success of King Kumärpäl was substantial.

Originally, Udayan was a simple merchant in a village named Vägharä near the town of Jälore, Rajasthan. He could hardly make ends meet and was passing his days in hardship. His wife Suhädevi suggested they move to a place with better economic prospects. During this time, King Siddharäj was ruling the state of Gujarat, and its prosperity was increasing by leaps and bounds. Hence Udayan thought about migrating to Gujarat.

At that time, King Siddharäj of Gujarat had built a new town named Karnävati (Amdäväd) in the memory of his father Karnadev. Since Karnävati was a fast growing city, Udayan decided to move there. He did not know anyone there so he first went to the local Jain temple. When Udayan arrived a religious lady named Lachchhi was worshipping in the temple. As she came out, she noticed the new young couple and asked them where they were from. Udayan replied that they were from Rajasthan and he was looking for some business in Karnävati.

Lachchhi was a compassionate lady. As she knew the newcomers were Jains, she took them home and treated them as her guests for a couple of days. Then she gave them an old house for shelter. Udayan settled there and started a small business. Luck favored him and within a short time he earned and saved enough to renovate the old house. While digging the ground, he came across a hidden treasure. Since he was honest, he took the treasure to Lachchhi and offered it to her because it belonged to her. She declined to accept it stating that since the property had been given to him, the treasure also belonged to him.

Udayan now had enough money to start a large-scale business. He made lots of money and in due course became the wealthiest man in Karnävati. The State also recognized his status and gave him the position of the first citizen of Karnävati. In that capacity, he rendered valuable service to the people of Karnävati.

At that time, the city of Khambhät (about 80 miles from Amdäväd) was the most lucrative seaport on the western coast of India. Politicians competed with one another to get the position of governor in that city. Due to the proven capability of Udayan he was appointed governor of Khambhät in 1120 A.D. He held that position for a fairly long period. Two major events have been attributed to him during his tenure as governor.

- At the suggestion of the queen mother, Minaldevi, he abolished the pilgrim tax of Bholad
- He helped Devchandra-suri to initiate a five-year old boy, Chängdev, who had the potential to shine as a great sage. (Later on Chängdev became the great Jain Ächärya Shri Hemchandra)

Shrävikä Lachchhi helping a Jain Shrävak

His loyalty to the king was unquestionable. He hesitated to help Kumärpäl who was roaming from town to town hiding from King Siddharäj. However, when Kumärpäl came to Khambhät in search of shelter, Hemchandra Ächärya advised Udayan to help him. Since Udayan highly respected the Ächärya, he agreed to hide Kumärpäl in his basement. Shortly thereafter, king Siddharäj died and Kumärpäl became king of Gujarat. King Kumärpäl kept Udayan in his position as governor of Khambhät and later brought him to Pätan (capital city of Gujarat) to work as his trusted advisor.

Udayan had not forgotten how religion had helped him during his bad times. He therefore used his wealth and position to promote Jainism. As a token of his devotion to the faith, he constructed several Jain temples. Three of them are recorded in Jain history. One was the temple known as Udayanvihär in Karnävati, another was Udävasahi in Dholkä (near by town of Karnävati), and the third one whose name is not recorded was in Khambhät.

During the later part of Udayan's life, Kumärpäl sent him to subdue Sumvar, a notorious bandit in the Saurashtra region. In that mission, he had to pass through Palitänä. He decided to go on a pilgrimage to Shatrunjay hill. To commemorate the pilgrimage, his statue has been erected on a camel's back in a small temple on the way to the main complex on the hill. That place is now mistakenly known as Päp Punya Ni Bäri (window of good and bad Karma).

At that time, there was a wooden temple on the hill. While Udayan was worshipping there, he saw a mouse take a lit wick in its mouth and roam about. Udayan recovered the wick from the mouse, but he realized that the temple could be set on fire by a mouse. He therefore vowed to construct a new temple there.

He succeeded in his expedition against Sumvar, but he was badly wounded in combat and his death was imminent. On his death bed he told his sons about his vow to reconstruct a new temple at Shatrunjay hill. They promised him that they would fulfill his vow. Thereafter, he died peacefully knowing his vow would be fulfilled.

Ämbad and Bähad:

Udayan had 4 sons, named Ämbad, Bähad, Chähad, and Sollak. Ämbad was a poet and a bold warrior. He became the chancellor of King Kumärpäl. He constructed the western walkway on Shatrunjay hill now known as Gheti Ni Päg. He expanded Udävasahi of Dholka and renovated the well-known temple of Shakunikävihär at Bharuch.

Ämbad had pledged his allegiance to Kumärpäl and served him with utmost sincerity and loyalty. When Kumärpäl's successor King Ajaypäl came to the throne, he began to undo everything Kumärpäl had stood for. As a result, Ämbad decided to resist him with all the means at his command. Ajaypäl sent troops to subdue him. Ämbad, however, refused to be subdued and died fighting Ajaypäl's troops.

The second son Bähad (also known as Vähad) was a politician and statesman. He first worked for King Siddharäj, and under King Kumärpäl's regime he became the king's trusted right hand person. When Kumärpäl undertook the renovation of Somnäth temple, the project was entrusted to Bähad who carried out the work very well.

In order to honor the pledge to his father, Bähad undertook the construction of a grand temple on Shatrunjay. The temple was completed in 1155 A.D. But soon after, portions of the temple fell down due to intense wind. Bähad then arranged to reconstruct the fallen parts so it could withstand high winds in the future.

There is an interesting anecdote associated with the construction of that temple. When Bähad undertook the work, many people wanted to contribute to the project. A list of donors was prepared in order to accommodate them. At that time, there was a poor man named Bhim who earned his livelihood going from place to place selling Ghee (refined butter). He went to the place where the list was being prepared. He had an intense desire to contribute to the project, but he had only one coin, the one he had earned that day. How could he speak about donating such a small amount when people were contributing thousands of coins? Bähad noticed his eagerness and called him to his side. He gently asked Bhim to contribute whatever he wanted. Naturally Bhim hesitated. Hesitatingly, he said that he wanted to contribute the coin he had earned that day.

Bähad not only accepted the offer, but also wrote Bhim's name at the top of the donors' list. When he was asked to explain, Bähad said that the other donors, including him, had contributed a part of their wealth while Bhim had contributed his entire wealth.

It so happened that when Bhim returned home his wife asked him to fix a wooden post to restrain their cow. As he was digging, he came across a box buried in the ground. As he opened it, he saw that it contained gold coins and other valuables. He thought it was the consequence of his contribution to the temple and took the entire wealth to Bähad as his contribution to the temple.

The construction project was completed in 1157 AD at a cost of 29.7 million coins and the opening ceremony was performed on a grand scale in the presence of Shri Hemchandra Ächärya.

The life story of Udayan, a religious and hard working Shrävak, is very inspiring to all of us. He was always humble and never forgot his benefactors. He raised brave and virtuous sons, Ämbad and Bähad, two gems of the Jain Sangha. Bhim's generosity is also praiseworthy. Bähad's act of putting Bhim's name at the top of the donors' list demonstrates his unbiased leadership and true understanding of religion.

34 Nobility of Savchand and Somchand

The Shatrunjay hill is a very sacred place of pilgrimage for Jains. It is located near the town of Palitänä, about 140 miles southwest of Amdäväd, Gujarat. There are nine temple complexes on the hill. They are popularly known as nine Tuks. One of them is Chaumukhaji Tuk, located on the peak of the hill. Here is an interesting story of the construction of the temple complex there.

During the latter part of the 16th century when King Akbar, the great Moghul king, was ruling over India there was a businessman named Savchand Jeram in the town of Vanthali in the Saurashtra region of Gujarat state. He owned a very large business. He had many ships that used to export goods to Indonesia and other countries. During these voyages, they would buy merchandise at one place and sell it at another for profit.

Once a fleet of 12 ships set sail with valuable merchandise. After selling all their goods at a foreign port, they were returning with valuable foreign merchandise. On the way back, the fleet encountered a heavy storm and had to wait on an island. Meanwhile, monsoons set in and the fleet was stranded on the island for a couple of months. Because the ships did not come back for a long time, Savchand's shipping agents made all possible efforts to locate them. Since they did not find any trace of the fleet, they reported to Savchand that the ships were lost.

This was a heavy loss to Savchand. He had invested a significant amount of money on the voyage and was expecting a handsome return by selling the merchandise that the ships were expected to bring back. With the loss of his ships, he faced an acute shortage of funds and it was hard for him to pay back his creditors. As the news about the lost ships spread, people started talking about how Savchand had lost everything and his creditors would have to write off their dues.

That set off a panic among his creditors. In order to realize their dues, they began to present their claims. Savchand was a highly religious and honest person. He tried to pay back his creditors as much as he could with the resources he had left. One of the creditors was the prince of Mängrol, a place not far from Vanthali. He had deposited Rs. 100,000 in Savchand's firm. That was a substantial amount because one rupee of that time would be worth about Rs. 250 today.

When the prince learned about the loss of Savchand's ships, he also became impatient and called for the repayment of his deposit. Savchand could not raise such a large amount so quickly. He requested the prince to wait while he tried to raise the money. The prince, however, insisted on getting the amount immediately. Savchand's name and credit were at stake. In order to maintain his credit, he had to find a way to pay the prince.

At that time, there was a businessman named Somchand Amichand in the city of Amdäväd. Savchand did not have any trade connection with him, but he had heard about Somchand's firm and knew Somchand to be a very noble gentleman. An idea occurred to him – he thought of satisfying the prince by giving him a promissory note which would be honored by Somchand's firm. The prince agreed to that form of payment. Savchand wrote a promissory note payable to the prince by Somchand's firm without Somchand's permission. Since he had no right to write this, he was overcome with sadness and guilt while preparing it and tears began to roll down his face. A few drops of his tears fell on the document and smeared the promissory note. Then, with a heavy heart Savchand handed the note to the prince and requested him to cash it with Somchand's firm.

The prince did not lose any time. He immediately proceeded towards Amdäväd and upon arriving presented the promissory note to Somchand's firm. The accountant took the note in his hand and asked his men to look for Savchand's account. The men searched their books, but they did not find any account in the name of Savchand. The men reported that Savchand had no trade connections with their firm. The accountant went to Somchand and informed him that he had received a promissory note of exchange from Savchand of Vanthali which, being unduly drawn, could not be honored.

Somchand was puzzled to learn that. He knew Savchand's firm by name and was aware that it was a well reputed business organization of Vanthali. He could not make out why Savchand would have drawn the note for such a large amount when Somchand did not have any trade links with his firm. He looked at the note again and noticed the letters smeared by Savchand's tears. He could make out from the water spots that Savchand must have been in a very embarrassing position and must have drawn the note out of sheer desperation.

It was clear to Somchand that Savchand had reposed trust in him by writing the note. It was now his turn to reciprocate. What good was his wealth if he could not extend a helping hand to a noble man in distress? He, therefore, decided to oblige and asked the accountant to honor the note. The accountant was confused and asked, "Which account should the amount be debited from?" Somchand instructed the accountant to debit it to his personal account.

Various incidences in the life of Savchand

The note was accordingly accepted, and the amount was paid to the prince. The prince did not actually need the money and had asked for payment because of his doubt about the financial stability of Savchand. When the note was honored, he felt reassured about Savchand's credibility and repented for insisting upon the return of his deposit. On his way home, he went to Savchand and told him that he had received the amount from Amdäväd. Savchand heartily thanked Somchand for that act of grace.

At the end of the monsoon, the ships resumed their return journey and safely returned with the merchandise. Savchand was very pleased and relieved. He made a huge fortune by selling the merchandise, and his prestige rose even higher than it was before the loss of his ships. It was now time for him to pay back Somchand. For that purpose, he personally went to Amdäväd and offered the amount of Rs. 100,000 with interest. Somchand, however, declined to accept it on the grounds that his books did not show any amount due from Savchand.

Savchand would not accept that. How could he go home without repaying the debt? He therefore pressed Somchand to accept the amount and said that he was willing to pay any amount that Somchand asked. Savchand added that if he failed to repay, he would feel guilty for drawing the undue promissory note. Somchand, however, replied that he had purchased the promissory note for the drops of tears. Those two drops of tears of a respectable man were worth Rs. 200,000 to him. Of that, he had paid only Rs. 100,000 to the prince and another Rs. 100,000 were still due to be paid. Saying this, he offered Rs. 100,000 to Savchand.

But how could Savchand accept that? He was indebted to Somchand for his graciousness in honoring the bill. For that grace Savchand was willing to pay any amount to Somchand. Instead of accepting the amount, Somchand was offering another Rs. 100,000 to him! As Savchand repeatedly insisted on repaying the amount of his promissory note, Somchand explained that he was unable to accept the amount because his books did not show any amount due from Savchand. In a way, he was right because the payment to the prince of Rs. 100,000 was debited to his personal account and not to Savchand's account.

In Rämäyan, there is an interesting event when neither Räm nor Bharat were willing to accept the throne, and they each asked the other to accept it. A similar dispute arose between Savchand and Somchand. Both of them offered a high payment to the other but neither of them was willing to accept the other's offer. Savchand continued to insist that Somchand accept the amount of his bill, but the latter would not only decline, but insisted on Savchand accepting another Rs. 100,000. At last, it was decided that they would refer the matter to the mediation of the Jain community (Sangha).

The executive committee of the Amdäväd Jain Sangha got together with both of them. After hearing them patiently, the Sangha concluded that since neither of them was ready to accept the amount offered by the other, the amount should be used for a noble cause. Both of them agreed and after making a substantial addition to the said amount, they decided to spend the money to construct a temple complex on Shatrunjay Hill. Accordingly, construction was undertaken in earnest. After completion, the opening ceremony of the complex was performed with great fanfare in 1619 A.D. In commemoration of their names, the complex is still known as Savä-Som Tuk.

Honesty in life as well as in business always pays off. The generosity of Somchand is praiseworthy. He did not take undue advantage of a person in distress; instead he helped an unknown person. Moreover, he did not expect anything in return.

Part VI
Contemporary Jain Legends

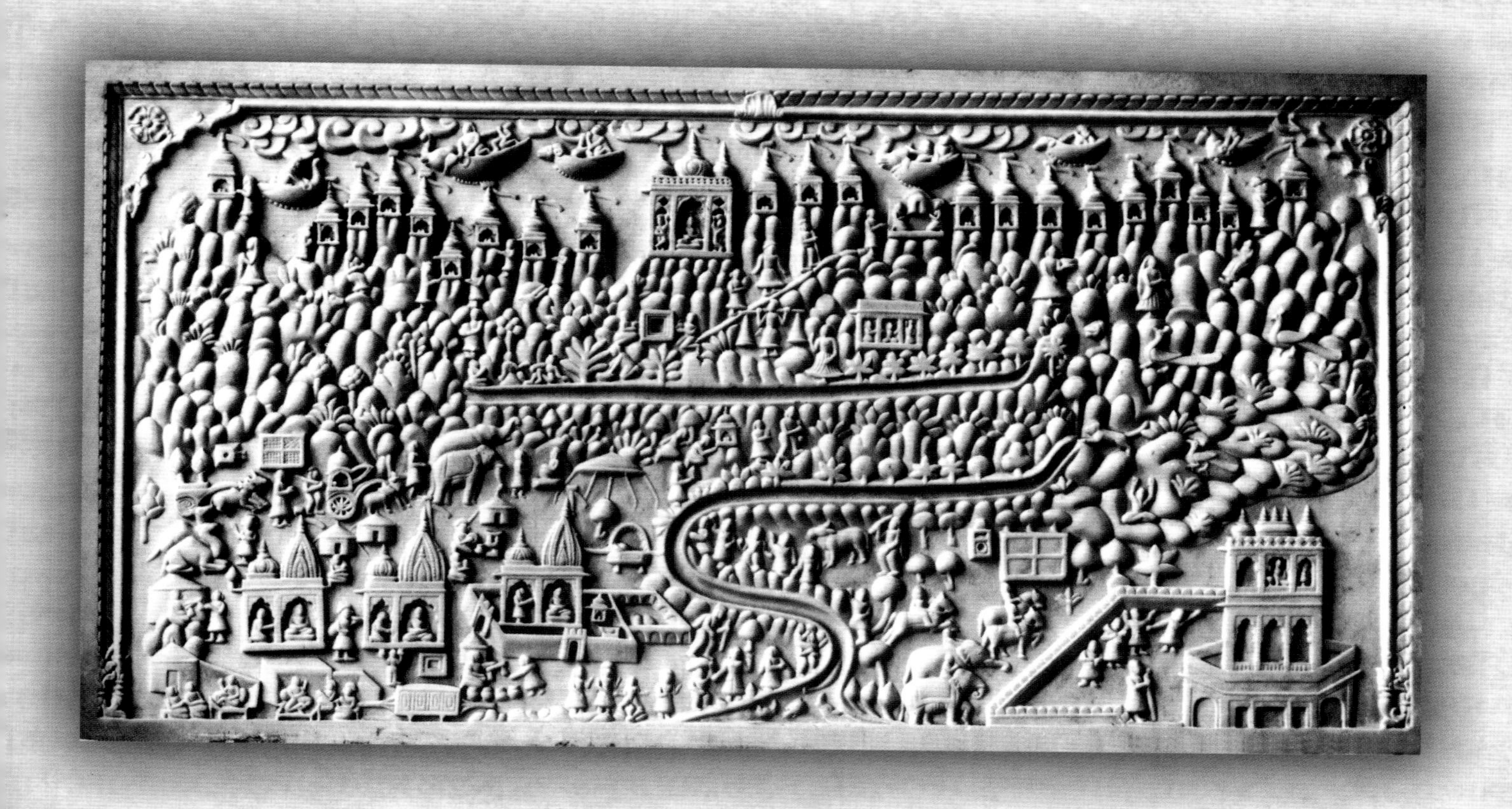

"Jain religion is not blind faith,
Nor is it emotional worship
inspired by fear or wonder.
It is the intuition of the
inherent purity of consciousness,
will and bliss of the self."
- Dr. Nathmal Tatia

35 Shrimad Räjchandra
(1867 - 1901)

Introduction:

Shrimad Räjchandra was a great seer and one of the most recognized Jain sages of modern times who has made priceless contributions to Jain philosophy and literature. He was a great philosopher, a brilliant poet, social reformer, thinker, and a self realized saint. Mahatma Gandhi was highly influenced by Shrimad's spiritual life. Shrimad's writings come from his experience of life and at present his teachings are widely followed by many Jain and Hindu aspirants seeking spiritual awakening and self realization.

Birth and Childhood:

Shrimad Räjchandra was born on the auspicious day of full-moon (Dev-Diwäli) of the month of Kärtik, 1924 V.S. (November 9, 1867) at Vaväniä, Morbi district, Gujarat State, India. His parents were Ravjibhai and Devabä. He was named Laxminandan at birth but after four years his name was changed to Raichand. Later he became famous by the name of Räjchandra.

Räjchandra's father and grandfather followed the Vaishnav (Hindu) religion. They were devotees of Lord Krishna. His mother, Devabä, was from a Jain family. Thus, the child Räjchandra was brought up under the unified culture of Jainism and Hinduism.

As a child, Räjchandra was deeply interested in reading various books. Once he read the Jain Pratikraman Sutras and was touched by the feelings of kindness to animals and the expression of sincere forgiveness from each other during daily Pratikraman ritual and Paryushan festival. He was drawn closer to the Jain faith because of the emphasis it places on self knowledge, self control, penance, renunciation and detachment from worldly affairs, and meditation. As a seeker of ultimate truth, Shrimad came to the conclusion that the philosophy and culture of Jain religion was of the highest order of truth and equanimity.

An incident that took place when he was 7 years old changed the course of his life. An adult acquaintance, Shri Amichandbhai died of a serpent-bite. Young Räjchandra asked his grandfather, "What does it mean to die?" His loving grandfather explained, "His soul has left the body and he will no longer be able to eat or talk or move. His body will be burnt outside the village." Räjchandra saw the dead body being burnt and slipped into deep contemplation. Suddenly as if a veil lifted and he recalled his past lives. With this experience he realized the pains of repeated births and deaths from one life to another. This incidence became a major spiritual awakening point in his life to free himself from the bondage of Karma and the life cycle of pain and misery.

Räjchandra started schooling at the age of seven. With his exceptional ability to remember exactly what he saw or heard or read once, he was able to complete the seven year elementary school education in a mere two years. The village school provided only seven years of education and hence his formal education came to an end. However, he continued to learn and read many books on his own. After his elementary education, he worked in his father's shop and conducted the business honestly and sincerely.

He composed his first poem at the age of eight and started writing poems and articles related to social issues for publication in the local newsletters. Despite his young age he wrote serious articles on social reform subjects like the need for improving female literacy rates, child marriages, and the display of wealth by the rich. He also composed poems with nationalistic zeal.

At a very young age, he had the supernatural ability to foresee what was likely to happen and he helped some people by saving them from possible disasters. By the time he was 18, he had become a very proficient astrologer. He was able to identify books merely by touching them and know the taste of food without tasting it. Along with developing all these extraordinary abilities, he became very compassionate towards all living beings and a strong promoter of non-violence.

Family:

At the age of 20, Räjchandra married Zabakben in 1888 AD (1944 V.S.). Zabakben was the daughter of Shri Popatlälbhai Jagjivandäs, the elder brother of Shri Reväshankarbhai who later became Shrimad's business partner. They had four children; two sons, Shri Chhaganläl and Shri Ratiläl and two daughters, Smt. Javalben and Smt. Käshiben. Shrimad had a younger brother, Shri Mansukhbhai.

Shrimad Räjchandra became a partner in a gemstone business in Mumbai at the age of 20 (1888 AD). He was absolutely ethical, honest, and very compassionate in all his business dealings. In a very short time his business flourished because of his wisdom and business insight. His regard for truth, adherence to high moral values, and firmness to do what was right inspired many others. In 1899 AD (1955 V.S.), he totally retired from business at the age of 31.

Power of Avadhän (Multi-tasking):

At the age of 17, Shrimad had observed someone performing eight different tasks simultaneously, known as Ashtä-vadhäni (eight tasks) in Gujarati. He studied the method and the next day he was able to perform twelve tasks. He soon improved his performance to be able to manage 52 Avadhäns or tasks. When he was 19, he was invited to perform his Avadhäns at a public meeting in Mumbai in the presence of the Bombay Chief Justice and other dignitaries. He successfully performed 100 Avadhäns (tasks) known as Shatävdhän.

The 100 tasks included a variety of activities like playing cards, playing chess, counting the bell chimes, completing mathematical manipulations like addition, division, and multiplication; composing poems with different themes and specified set of words, arranging the order of words from 16 different languages which included English, Greek, Latin and Arabic (note that Shrimad's formal study included only Gujarati up to Grade 7 of elementary school).

This was an unbelievable feat and the performance was given much publicity in all the major newspapers like the Times of India and Pioneer. Shrimad was invited to go to Europe and demonstrate his extraordinary talents. This would have meant more fame and substantial material gain. However, he declined the offer because it would be extremely difficult to stay in Europe as per Jain religious standards and also he would be distracted from his main objective of spiritual progress.

By the time he was 20, his fame had spread throughout India and he realized that he was achieving only material benefits for his amazing powers and that was not what he wanted from his life. He gave up all such activities completely and only concentrated on self restraint, detachment from worldly matters, contemplation, and meditation to progress spiritually so that he could free himself from the cycles of births and deaths.

Shrimad's Writings:

In his early years, Shrimad composed poems and articles on social reforms arousing nationalistic passion. When he was working in his father's shop, he had done an in-depth study of Jain Ägams and scriptures after having learnt Sanskrit and Präkrit languages on his own at the age of 14.

At the age of 16, he wrote Moksha-mälä and its compendium Bhävanä-bodh, which literally means 'garland of liberation'. True to its name, it deals with subjects that lead towards the path of liberation. It is written in a simple and easy to understand language, but explains the Jain religion in finest detail. Its 108 lessons were composed in three days!

Shrimad Räjchandra writing Ätmasiddhi-shästra
Standing from Left: Shri Laghuräj Swämi, Shri Sobhagbhai and Shri Ambälälbhai (with lantern)

Ätmasiddhi-shästra is an epic poem and prime jewel composed by Shrimad in Gujarati in 1896 while he was in Nadiad, a town near Ahmedäbäd. On one auspicious evening, he composed 142 stanzas of Ätmasiddhi-shästra in one sitting of less than 90 minutes. The fact that Shrimad composed such comprehensive and all inclusive work within such a short time can only give us a clue of the depth of spiritual wealth he possessed.

The subject matter of Ätmasiddhi-shästra is the scientific characterization of the six fold modes of Soul, its existence, its eternity, doer of its karma, the impact of Karma on it, the nature of the pure consciousness (liberation), and its potential for attaining liberation from Karma. It describes the Jain philosophy comprehensively and also shows how Anekäntaväda allows Jainism to encompass all other Indian faiths. Many scholars have written an elegant commentary on the Ätmasiddhi-shästra.

Apurva-avasar is his last major compilation. It is the most divine poem in which Shrimad expresses the fourteen stages of spiritual progress for ultimate liberation. Apurva-avasar was incorporated in the Prayer book in Gandhiji's Ashram.

The complete works of Shrimad containing more than thirty five poems and close to 950 letters, written to various people who came in contact with him, are compiled in a text called "Vachanämrit". A high level of spirituality is evident in his writings. If one delves deeper into his literature, one will notice that his writings provide excellent discourses for attaining self realization leading to liberation.

Mahatma Gandhi was very highly impressed by Shrimad's divinity, and the way he led his life. He accepted Shrimad as his spiritual guide with great respect and reverence. When Gandhiji was in South Africa, he was under intense pressure from his Christian and Muslim friends to adopt their faith. He wrote to Shrimad for guidance. Shrimad's guidance convinced him of how his own faith, Hinduism, would ensure his spiritual progress. Gandhiji has written reverently about Shrimad in his autobiography and has paid glorious tribute to him on several occasions. He often revealed that he learnt compassion for all beings and non-violence from Shrimad. According to him, Shrimad's life and spiritual writings impacted him more than Tolstoy and Ruskin.

Spiritual Progress:

Shrimad did not have a spiritual teacher in his life. At the age of 7 when he was able to recall his past lives, he clearly remembered his association with Lord Mahävir in a previous life.

In 1891 A.D. (1947 V.S.) at the age of 23, Shrimad realized Samyak Darshan (Right Faith or Intuition). He continued to enhance his progress by slowly detaching himself from the material world, deeply studying scriptures, strengthening virtues, refraining from worldly pleasures, and remaining in meditation for longer duration. He started to stay at lonely places outside Mumbai for more than a month at a time. In the beginning there were many obstacles in his way because he needed to perform his duties as a house holder and as a businessman.

From 1896 A.D. (1952 V.S.), he often spent several months in isolation in the woods of Uttarsanda, Idar, and Kavitha where he would eat only one meal during the day and sleep very little. He spent his time in deep meditation and attained a highly enlightened state of self realization at the age of 28.

He retired totally from business at the age of 31 in 1899 A.D. (1955 V.S.) and requested his mother to permit him to renounce the worldly life permanently to become a monk, which his mother denied out of love and affection. However, after two years of clever persuasion, he was hopeful of his mother's permission but by this time his health deteriorated and he did not recover his health. He died in 1901 A.D. in Rajkot at the very young age of thirty three.

Followers:

Though Shrimad had tried to keep his spiritual personality completely private, several people accepted him as their guide to achieve ultimate liberation and devoted their lives to him. Some of his closest followers were:

Shri Sobhagbhai:

Almost 350 of the 950 letters of Shrimad Räjchandra were written to Shri Sobhagbhai who was about 40 years older than him. In the very first meeting, Sobhagbhai recognized Shrimad as a highly self realized person and accepted him as his true guru. He was simple in his behavior and serious in devotion. He was a native of Saila, a town near Rajkot. Based on his request, Shrimad composed the epic poem Ätmasiddhi-shästra so that it would be easier to memorize. Shri Sobhagbhai attained self realization and died in deep meditation (Samädhi).

Shri Laghuräj Swämi:

Shri Laghuräj Swämi was a Sthänakaväsi Jain monk and one of most devoted disciples of Shrimad. As a monk, his devotion to Shrimad caused him great problems from the Jain community.

Shri Laghuräj Swämi attained self realization during Shrimad's presence and then established the Agäs Äshram, near Vadodara. The Äshram can take credit for preserving Shrimad's writings and making it available to the Jain community at large. Agäs is an important place for Shrimad's followers. Today there are more than fifty Äshrams in India and aboard where the followers worship and study Shrimad's literature based on the divine faith and testimony provided by Shri Laghuräj Swämi.

Shri Ambälälbhai:

Ambälälbhai, a native of Khambhat, was a very devoted disciple who sacrificed a brilliant legal career to be in the service of Shrimad. Shrimad entrusted him to copy scriptural works and his letters because of his exceptional memory. He and Shrimad's younger brother, Mansukhbhai, were responsible for recovering Shrimad's letters and writings and publishing them. Four years after Shrimad, in 1905 A.D. (1961 V.S.), Ambälälbhai attained self realization and passed away in deep Samädhi at a very young age.

Shri Joothäbhai:

Joothäbhai was the first person to recognize Shrimad's divinity and accepted him as his spiritual mentor. Their relationship was very close but also very short as Shri Joothäbhai passed away when he was only 23 years old in 1890 A.D. (1946 V.S.).

Teachings and Contribution of Shrimad Räjchandra:

All of Shrimad's literature is based on Bhagawän Mahävir's teachings. He presented these teachings, in simple Gujarati and Hindi, in prose and poetry forms. As we study Shrimad's writings in depth, we find that he has made an enormous effort to shed new light on true spirituality. He has succeeded in reforming the blind faith with real spiritual awakening.

His biggest contribution is to point out the mistakes most people make in following a teacher based on the external conduct and dress code. The spiritual journey led by a wrong teacher leads the disciple to extended life cycles of misery and pain. On the other hand, when an aspirant is able to know and follow the teachings of a true teacher (Sadguru), he will be able to attain true freedom and liberation.

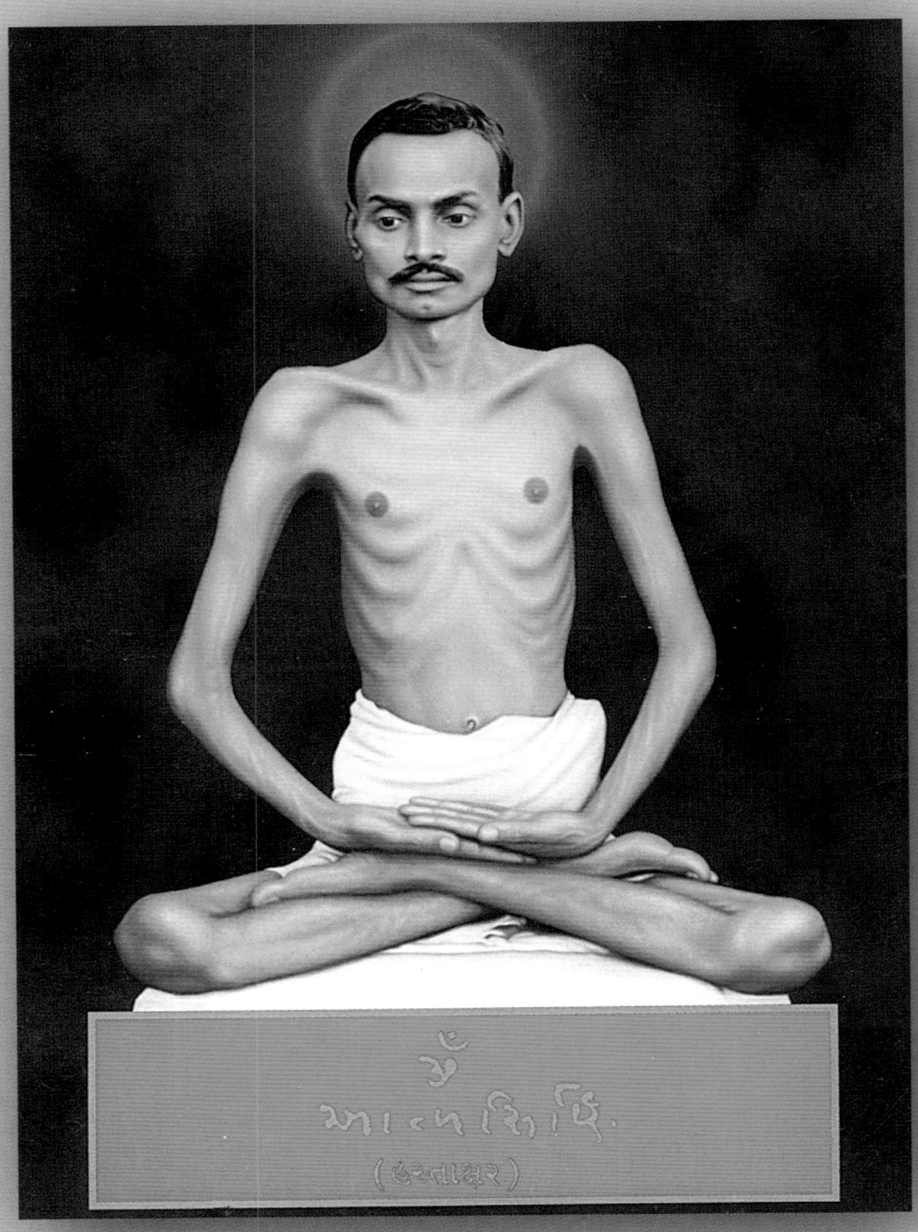

Shrimad Räjchandra

1. Morality:

Good manners, good activities, and good behavior are the roots of holiness.

All living beings are seen as equal. Therefore, do not cause pain to any soul, nor extort work from any soul beyond their ability and capacity.

2. Human life:

All living beings long for permanent happiness and there is no exception to this. This desire can be fulfilled only in a human life. Yet human beings choose unhappiness. This is due to his illusionary state (Mohaniya Karma - Mithyätva) in which he sees happiness in worldly desires and possessions.

3. Non-attachment to Worldly Affairs (Vairägya)

Detachment from worldly and materialistic affairs and family relationships is defined as Vairägya and achieving it is essential for eternal happiness.

True renunciation is always followed by the true knowledge of the self or the soul. Without true renunciation, a person will not be able to gain the true knowledge of the soul. If one stops only at the stage of renunciation and there is no desire for true knowledge, his/her human life would be in vain.

4. Knowledge and Wisdom:

Through proper knowledge, we are able to know the forms and qualities of the substances of the universe.

The Jain scripture, Uttarädhyayan Sutra, indicates that "Knowledge is like a needle with thread. Just like a needle with thread in it does not get lost; a person with knowledge, will not lose the right religious path in this world."

It is the true knowledge with which (a) an external feeling is controlled; (b) attachment for life, family and worldly pleasures decreases and (c) a true truth is revealed.

If you know yourself (your true nature), you know the whole world; if you do not know yourself, your knowledge is worthless.

Conclusion:

Shrimad Räjchandra was a great saint and a self realized Master, an outstanding educationist, a born poet, possessed an extra-ordinary power of memory, a reformer of society, a keen follower and an advocate of non-violence and had equal respect for all religions.

As with many great personalities, Shrimad's greatness was not recognized in his life time. Shrimad was not popular among Jains because he spoke about the faults in Jain society and the traditions being carried out without understanding the proper meaning and purpose behind them. Many people have recognized his greatness after his death.

Shrimad has put great emphasis on the need of a Sadguru (true teacher) in one's life for spiritual progress and ultimately to attain liberation.

Shrimad always maintained that since he had not taken the vow of dikshä (sainthood), he was not eligible to preach the path of liberation. Therefore, even with his wealth of knowledge, he did not preach to the masses. He hoped that later in his life, he would become a monk and when the time was right, he could bring the proper teachings of Jainism to the masses, as there were many undesired factors in the practice of Jainism at that time.

Shrimad's writings to his close associates and his personal notes are the essence of Jain religion. He has given us priceless spiritual gifts including Mokshamälä, Ätmasiddhi-shästra, Apurva Avasar and many other spiritual writings in the form of letters, articles, and poems. In his short life of 33 years, he has delivered the spiritual message of eternal importance. He explained Bhagawän Mahävir's teachings in simple words. Now these teachings have become accessible to ordinary people and we have the unique opportunity to learn about the inner state of a truly self realized person.

36 Virchand R. Gandhi

A Brief Summary of his Life and Mission

(August 25, 1864 to August 7, 1901)

It was the memorable day of September 11, 1893. The Columbus Hall of the Art Institute of Chicago was overflowing with more than 3,000 delegates of different nations and religions. It was the opening day of the Parliament of World Religions Conference, the first such conference ever organized in the history of mankind. The aim of the conference was to impart to the world, the knowledge of different religions, to promote a feeling of fraternity between followers of diverse religious persuasions, and to pave the way for world peace. The conference lasted for 17 days.

Two young men among them, with their Indian costumes and turbans drew special attention from the public - one was the world famous Swämi Vivekänanda, who represented Hinduism and the other was Shri Virchand Räghavji Gandhi who represented Jainism. They made such an impact at the Parliament of Religions with their impressive speeches and personality that both of them were requested to prolong their stay in the USA and continued to give speeches at different cities after the conference was over.

Shri Virchand Gandhi, a young man of twenty-nine, impressed the delegates not only by his eloquence, but also by the sheer weight of his scholarship. The impartiality of his outlook and the oratorical skill of this man fascinated the delegates at the conference. An American newspaper wrote, "Of all eastern scholars, it was this youth whose lecture on Jain faith and conduct was listened to with great interest attention."

Shri Virchand R. Gandhi was born on August 25, 1864 in Mahuva, near Bhavanagar, Gujarat, India. After his primary and secondary education in Bhavanagar, he joined Elphinstone College in Mumbai. He graduated and obtained a B.A. Degree with honors from the University of Bombay in 1884. He was probably the first graduate amongst the Jains at that time. He was also a student of Buddhism, Vedanta Philosophy, Yoga, Christianity and Western philosophy. He had also done a comparative study of various philosophies, which equipped him for talks on various subjects with confidence. He had command over fourteen languages including Gujarati, Hindi, Bengali, English, Präkrit, Sanskrit, and French.

Shri Gandhi became the first honorary secretary of the Jain Association of India in 1885 at the age of 21. As secretary, he worked very hard for the abolition of poll tax levied on pilgrims to Mount Shatrunjay, the most sacred place of Jain religion at Palitänä, Gujarat, India. In those days to protest against the ruler was to invite severe punishment and even death. He prepared a case to compromise. He made a strong representation to Lord Ray, the governor of Bombay, and Colonel Watson, the political agent and eventually abolished the poll tax in place of a fixed payment of Rs. 15,000 per year to the ruler for looking after the safety of the pilgrims and the holy place.

In 1891 Mr. Boddam, an Englishman set up a factory for slaughtering pigs and making tallow out of them at Mount Sametshikhar, another holy place of Jain pilgrimage near Calcutta, in the state of Bihar, India. Shri Virchand Gandhi went all the way to Calcutta to stop the killing of pigs at the holy place. He stayed there for six months, learned Bengali, prepared his case against the factory, and ultimately got this verdict issued: "Sametshikhar is a place of Jain pilgrimage and nobody else has any right to interfere there." He got the factory to close down.

Virchand Gandhi

Shri Virchand Gandhi was a great social reformer at a very young age. At the very young age of 22, he wrote long essays to remove evil social customs and continuously fought against it and was successful in eradicating some of them.

Shri Virchand Gandhi sailed to USA along with Swämi Vivekänanda to attend the Parliament of World Religion Conference in 1893. He stayed in USA for about two years after the conference and gave lectures in cities such as Chicago, Boston, New York, and Washington. He also visited England, France, Germany and other places in Europe. In foreign countries he wore a long and loose kurta, a white shawl on his shoulder, a golden bordered Kathiawadi turban on his head, and country shoes. This external appearance bore the imprint of India. He delivered more than 535 lectures on Jainism, Yoga, Indian systems of philosophy, Indian culture, occultism, and spiritualism. He qualified as a Barrister in London at one of the Inns of the Court but did not use this qualification for monetary gain.

Virchand Gandhi talked about the doctrines of Jainism in such a coherent manner that some newspapers published the text of his lecture in full. He had a most effective way of handling the otherwise difficult terminology of Jainism. He had an extraordinary ability to clarify his statements in a consistent and logical manner. At the conference, he made a brief but striking presentation on the fundamentals of Jain religion. He expounded Jain religion in its main aspects namely: Jain philosophy, Jain way of life, and Jain code of conduct.

Another special characteristic of Shri Virchand Gandhi's lectures on Jain religion was that they did not deal in criticism of other religions. Free from sectarian preferences and prejudices, his impartial ideology is an apt expression of the Jain who practices non-violence (Ahimsa) in life and pluralistic views (Anekäntaväda) in thoughts. His discourses convinced the elite of America of the fact that Jain religion has an authentic and rational religious tradition. His speeches received extensive publication in several leading newspapers.

Shri Virchand Gandhi was a great exponent of Indian culture and religion, besides being a brilliant scholar of Jainism. His speeches at the parliament echoed the true spirit and culture of India. The prevailed belief in America was that India was a country of tigers, serpents, magicians, and kings. Christian missionaries also presented a distorted picture of the people of India. Shri Virchand Gandhi and Swämi Vivekänanda made a great effort to give the people abroad the true perspective on India. Explaining the importance of Indian culture to foreigners, he said, "It is an astonishing fact that foreigners have been constantly attacking India and in the face of all those aggressions the soul of India has stood vital and watchful. Her conduct and religion are safe and the whole world looks at India with a steady gaze."

Shri Virchand Gandhi was not a dogmatic person. He spoke as a Jain but he forcefully defended Hinduism from the attack of Westerners at the Parliament. Above all, he was first Indian then Jain. He was accorded a warm reception and shown the highest appreciation from clubs, literary and church societies, philosophical branches, and spiritual associations in USA and other countries. His lectures also served to educate the Western society regarding the salient features of Indian culture.

Five decades before the independence of India, Virchand Gandhi had a prophetic vision. He said in one of his lectures, "You know my brothers and sisters, that we are not an independent nation, we are subjects of Her Gracious Majesty Queen Victoria the 'defender of the faith', but if we are a nation in all that the name implies with our own government and our own rulers, with our laws and institutions controlled by us free and independent, I affirm that we should seek to establish and for ever maintain peaceful relations with all the nations of the world."

Virchand Gandhi was not only a philosophical thinker but he also had the welfare of the nation at heart. He collected a shipload of grain and about Rs. 40,000 ($10,000) cash for famine relief in India in 1896 while he was in USA.

In America, Virchand Gandhi founded various societies, such as:

- The Gandhi Philosophical Society
- The School of Oriental Philosophy
- The Society for the Education of Women of India

The secretary of the latter institution was Mrs. Howard who had adopted pure vegetarianism, practiced Sämäyika daily, and followed other codes of conduct of Jainism. In England, he founded the Jain Literature Society and taught Jainism there. Mr. Herbert Warren, a religious enthusiast, abandoned non-vegetarianism and adopted the Jain religion. He summarized Virchand Gandhi's lectures and published a book known as 'Herbert Warren's Jainism.'

The following literature was published by Shri Virchand R. Gandhi or complied from his speeches:

Title	Year Published	Language	Pages
Jaina Philosophy	1907	English	375
Karma Philosophy	1913	English	221
Yoga Philosophy	1912/1993	English	309
The Systems of Indian Philosophy	1970/1993	English	188
Selected speeches of V. R. Gandhi	1963	English	85
Religion and Philosophy of Jains	1993	English	264
Essay - Radvä Kutväni Hanikärak Chäl	1886	Gujarati	37
Concentration – 12 Lectures on Meditation	1916	English	64
The Unknown Life of Jesus Christ	1894	English	128
Savirya Dhyäna	1902/1989	Gujarati	158
Herbert Warren's Jainism	1961/1983	English	164

While he was in England, his health suddenly took a turn for the worse. He returned to India, but a few weeks later Shri Virchand Gandhi passed away at the very young age of 37 in Bombay on August 7, 1901. He rendered an excellent service to India and Jainism by interpreting Indian culture and religion in its true spirit to the western world. He was a brilliant promising young man, full of hopes and aspirations of service to his religion and community. His name will continue to be remembered as a great champion of Jain religion and of Indian culture.

Part VII
Moral Stories

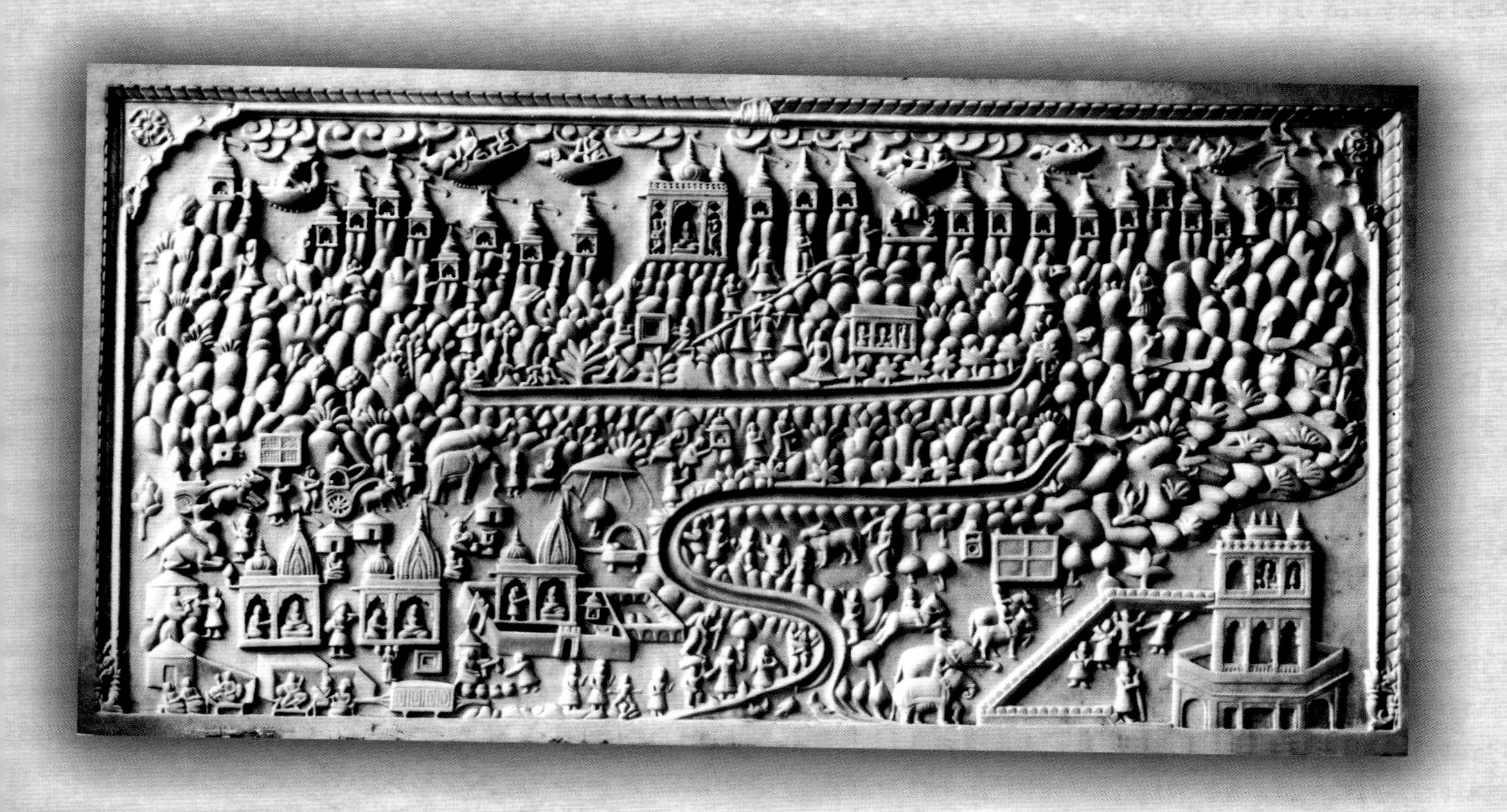

"Meditation is the best way of regression from all transgressions"

- Niyamasära (65)

37 King Hansa

In the city of Räjpur, there lived a king named Hansa. He was a fair and just king, known for his devotion to truth and non-violence. On top of Mount Ratnasringa, there was a beautiful temple dedicated to Rishabhadev, the first Tirthankar. During the month of Chaitra, on the day of the full moon, people came from far to visit and worship at the temple. Once, the king decided to visit the temple. He asked his council of ministers to look after the kingdom during his prolonged absence and left with members of the royal household on this spiritual mission.

A few days after king Hansa departed, king Arjun attacked the city. In spite of putting up a strong fight, king Hansa's army was defeated, and many of the generals lost their lives on the battlefield. King Arjun gained control of the palace and the treasury. King Arjun occupied the royal throne and enforced his authority over the entire kingdom.

King Hansa heard the story of their defeat on the way to the temple. The king's courtiers were very upset and advised him to return to the city. The king said, "I have given up control of the kingdom, and we are on a spiritual mission and that is what we should be thinking about. So let us keep going to the temple." The king's courtiers were unhappy about the king's decision and worried about the safety of their families at home. One by one, they all dropped out until only one umbrella bearer was left with the king.

On the way to the temple, they had to pass through the forest. The king took off his royal dress and jewelry and gave them to his servant. While passing through the forest, the servant was separated from the king.

As the king was walking, a deer ran in front of him and disappeared. Right after that, a hunter came running with a bow in his hand and asked the king if he had seen the deer. The king knew that if he told the truth, the deer would be killed. He decided not to answer the question and instead kept talking about irrelevant things. He said that he came from Räjpur. The hunter asked him again about the deer, and he answered that he was the king. The hunter was very upset with his answers and left in anger.

King Hansa avoiding the hunter's question to protect a deer

By now, the king was tired and decided to rest under a tree. He overheard a discussion in the bushes about robbing some monks who would pass that way in the next two days. The king got concerned about the safety of the monks. While he was thinking about what he could do, some policemen approached him and asked if he had seen any suspicious people that looked like robbers. They said, "These people are very dangerous and we have heard that they harm holy people. We are here to arrest them or even shoot them if necessary to protect the holy people."

King Hansa overhearing the robbers secretly talking in the bushes

The king was in a dilemma again whether to tell the truth or not. He was concerned that if he told the police about the robbers, they would be harmed and if he did not, the monks would be harmed. He thought, "If by telling the truth someone gets harmed or killed, then telling that truth is not the best choice. Truth is supposed to protect and not harm anyone. He said, "My friends, you are asked to guard the monks. Why not go and look after the monks and worry about the robbers if they confront the monks." The policemen agreed and left to join the monks.

The robbers who were hiding in the bushes heard all this. They were amazed at the mercy shown by this stranger. They came out, thanked him for saving their lives, and told him that they were at his service. The king advised them, "My dear friends, give up harassing people, the fugitive life you lead and be good citizens." The robbers promised that they would not harm the monks anymore and would try to be good citizens.

As if this was not enough, a group of soldiers came and asked him if he had seen king Hansa. The king asked, "What do you want from King Hansa?" They explained that they were the trusted men of King Arjun and they had been told to arrest King Hansa and kill him, and if they did they would receive a big reward. King Hansa thought for a moment and said, "I am King Hansa. Carry out your duty as told by your king." After saying that, he closed his eyes, stood in meditation, and started reciting the Namaskär Mantra.

King Hansa disclosing the truth despite of danger to his life

At once, a dev (demigod / angel) appeared and said, "Oh, king! I am overwhelmed by your truthfulness and compassion. I have captured King Arjun, made him a prisoner, and have given control of your kingdom back to your ministers. Today is a great day for worship, but the temple is too far from here. There is no way you can reach there in time. My chariot is at your service. Please let me take you there."

King Hansa was surprised by the miraculous turn of events. In the company of the dev (demigod / angel), he reached the summit of Mount Ratnasringa in time to worship. The demigod then escorted him back to his kingdom. King Hansa pardoned King Arjun and released his soldiers immediately. The angel appointed four lieutenants to look after the safety of the king and his kingdom and then departed. King Hansa once again ruled the city of Räjpur and the people were happy.

The main theme here is the importance of the Jain principles of truthfulness and non-violence, and their interrelationship. Sometimes, following one Jain principle blindly can lead to the violation of another principle, which is what King Hansa was faced with on multiple occasions. He thought about each situation carefully and found a very creative, smart, and beneficial solution without violating any principles and without hurting anyone. This showed his devotion and adherence to Jainism. When faced with Arjun's soldiers in the last situation, he told the truth since no other people or principles were involved, even though it meant the end of his life. He once again stuck to his Jain principles, even though he might have been killed for it.

38 Kamalsen

Shripat Sheth and his wife Sundari once visited Shri Shilandhar Ächärya and told him that both of them observed daily vows such as reciting Namaskär Mantra and performing Navakärashi (to eat 48 minutes after sunrise), Sämäyika (meditation for 48 minutes), but their son, Kamalsen, did not observe any vows.

Kamalsen's parents were unhappy and anxious about their son's lack of devotion and spirituality. They requested the monk to give some advice to their son, so that he would change for the better and be happy in this life as well as the next. The monk willingly obliged.

After reaching home, the merchant said to his son, "Well, my son, a great teacher is visiting our town. He is a very learned man, and his lectures are worth listening to." The next day, they accompanied their son to the lecture. After paying their respect to the Ächärya, they sat down to listen. The Ächärya talked about many things, including hell, heaven, misery, and Keval-jnän. After the discourse, the parents asked Kamalsen what he felt about the lecture. Kamalsen replied, "I was too busy watching the movements of the Ächärya's neck area." His parents were greatly dismayed and returned home disappointed.

Kamalsen watching the potter hiding the treasure

Soon after, another great sage, Ächärya Gunasägar-suri, visited the town and his parents and Kamalsen went to visit him. The Ächärya told the audience various stories of bravery, humor, sorrow, and family relations with religious messages because such stories attract common people. The boy liked those stories so everyday he attended the Ächärya's sermons and listened with interest. After a few days, the Ächärya was preparing to leave town. Kamalsen joined the people at the farewell ceremony. Many people pledged to observe some vow. Kamalsen was asked if he would take a vow. He said, "I will not tell a lie except during the day or the night. I will not put a whole watermelon into my mouth, nor will I eat cow manure." The Ächärya was surprised by the boy's ridiculous behavior. Hence, in order to repent, the boy vowed not to eat food without looking at the baldhead of Simelo, a potter in the town. The Ächärya was very pleased with Kamalsen for taking a vow even though it was a very strange one.

One day, Simelo went to the forest to get some clay. Kamalsen was about to eat lunch when his mother reminded him of his vow. He immediately ran to the forest to find the bald potter. There he saw the potter digging in the ground. While digging, the potter came across a pot full of gems and precious stones. At the boy's arrival, he started hiding it underneath a heap of soil. Kamalsen shouted, "Yes! I have seen it (indicating to himself that he had seen the bald head of the potter, as per his vow)." The potter thought Kamalsen meant that he saw the pot and he did not want anyone else to know about the gems. Therefore, he told the boy that he would share half the treasure from the pot if he did not tell anyone. At first, Kamalsen did not understand what Simelo was talking about but later he understood and gladly accepted the treasure and returned home.

Kamalsen thought deeply as he returned home, "A simple vow taken as a joke brought me this wealth. Had I taken this vow seriously, I would have benefited a lot more." This incident changed Kamalsen's life. He then observed many vows and became very happy.

When one takes vows to do something, it should require true devotion and discipline and require some form of sacrifice consistent with the principles of Jainism. Taking vows that do not fit this profile is useless and has no meaning. Taking vows and following through with them benefits one's soul. These benefits may be evident in one's present life or may not be evident until some future birth. However, vows definitely help to discipline your present life.

39 Vipul and Vijan

In the forests of Pratisthän, there lived a hermit well known for predicting future events. Many times the people of the village gathered around him asking for predictions, even though the hermit did not always like to satisfy their curiosity. The hermit kept moving deeper and deeper into the jungle until people stopped looking for him. Two friends, Vipul and Vijan got lost in the jungle on their way to Pratisthän. They feared for their lives in the dark and looked for shelter. Late in the night, they saw a hut and approached it with fear and uneasiness. They peeped into the hut and saw a hermit deep in meditation. They assumed that he was the hermit known for his predictions. They waited until the hermit completed his meditation and then told him their story about getting lost in the forest.

The hermit heard their story and offered them fruits. The compassionate hermit told them to rest. The next morning the hermit requested one of his disciples to show them the way to the village. However, before Vipul and Vijan left, they folded their hands and asked the hermit to tell them their future. The hermit declined politely, telling them that it was not advisable to know their future and sometimes predictions may prove to be wrong. Both friends insisted and at last, the hermit told them their future. He looked at Vipul and told him he would become a king within a year while Vijan would die at the hands of an assassin during the same time.

Vipul and Vijan asking a hermit about their future

Outside the forest, Vipul could not contain his joy while Vijan was very gloomy. It was only natural. Back in their town, Vipul behaved arrogantly and told everyone that if they misbehaved he would chop off their heads when he became king. Everyone in the village was afraid of him. Meanwhile Vijan, a teacher, went about his work with great devotion and spent a lot of his time in prayers and social work. He was humble to all and eventually overcame his sadness. He no longer feared death, but also surrendered himself to his destiny.

Change of destiny because of the good deeds of Vijan and bad deeds of Vipul

Six months later, Vipul asked Vijan to accompany him to select the site of his future palace. Both were surveying a deserted region when Vipul stumbled across a pot full of gold coins. He was joyous and told Vijan that he was going to use the money to buy a crown. Right then, a robber jumped out of the bushes and tried to snatch the pot. Vijan came to his friend's rescue, and the robber attacked him with a dagger. Vijan was experienced in defensive tactics and drove off the robber, although he received a cut on the shoulder. The grateful Vipul offered his friend half the gold but Vijan politely refused saying he was going to die soon and would have no use for the gold. Vipul spent the money irrationally and squandered it in eating and drinking. A full year passed; Vipul did not become a king, and Vijan did not die.

Both friends went back to the hermit in search of an explanation. The hermit was in meditation. He said to Vipul, "Your destiny changed because of your thoughtless actions over the year. The crown that was meant to come to you was reduced to a simple pot of gold which you found in the field." He said to Vijan,

"Your prayers, humility, and trust in religion changed your destiny too. Death by the hands of an assassin was changed to a mere wound." The two friends returned to the village thoughtful of their actions and the results, and the meaning of life.

One's destiny is driven by one's Karma. In turn, one's Karma is governed by one's thoughts and deeds in the current as well as past lives. Knowing their fate, Vipul and Vijan changed their behavior - One changed for the worse, and the other for the better. Arrogance and materialistic indulgence led to bad Karma that impacted Vipul's future in a negative manner. Conversely, humility, prayers, and faith in the divine led to good Karma which impacted Vijan's future in a positive manner. We should all strive to behave in a manner that will promote good Karma in our current and future lives.

40 Two Frogs

A group of frogs were playing in the farm, when two of them fell into a pot of milk. All the other frogs gathered around the pot to see what could be done to help their companions. When they saw how deep the pot was, they agreed that it was hopeless and told the two frogs in the pot that they should prepare themselves for their fate, because they were as good as dead.

Unwilling to accept this terrible fate, the two frogs began to jump with all of their might. Some of the frogs shouted into the pot that it was hopeless, and that the two frogs wouldn't be in that situation if they had been more careful, and more responsible. The other frogs continued sorrowfully shouting that they should save their energy and give up, since they were already as good as dead. The two frogs continued jumping with all their might, and after a while, were quite weary. Finally, one of the frogs took heed to the calls of his fellow frogs. Exhausted, he quietly resolved himself to his fate, drowned to the bottom of the pot, and died.

The other frog continued to jump as hard as he could, although his body was wracked with pain and he was quite exhausted. Once again, his companions began yelling for him to accept his fate, stop the pain and just die. The weary frog jumped harder and harder and, wonder of wonders, the milk turned into butter with all the movement of the jumping. The frog was now able to stand on the layer of butter on top, use that as leverage and finally leaped so high that he sprang out of the pot. Amazed, the other frogs celebrated his freedom and then gathering around him asked, "Why did you continue jumping when we told you it was impossible?" The astonished frog explained to them that he was deaf, and as he saw their gestures and shouting, he thought they were cheering him on. What he had perceived as encouragement inspired him to try harder and to succeed against all odds.

The book of Proverbs says, "There is death and life in the power of the tongue". Your encouraging words can lift someone up and help them make it through the day. Your destructive words can cause deep wounds; they may be the weapons that destroy someone's desire to continue trying - or even their life. Your destructive, careless word can diminish someone in the eyes of others, destroy their influence and have a lasting impact on the way others respond to them. Be careful what you say. Speak life to (and about) those who cross your path. There is enormous power in words. If you have words of kindness, praise or encouragement - speak them now to, and about, others. Listen to your heart and respond.